Let's hop

my dear Rachel,

Avideh

May 2021

Terror In The Name Of God

Mykonos restaurant, [Police archives]
From right to left: Sadegh Sharafkandi, Homayoun Ardalan and Fatah Abdoli

Terror In The Name Of God

| Parviz Dastmalchi |
| Translated by Avideh Motmaen-Far |

MEHRI PUBLICATION

Research * 40

Terror In The Name Of God

Parviz Dastmalchi
Translated by **Avideh Motmaen-Far**

British Library Cataloguing Publication Data:
A catalogue record for this book is available from
the British Library | ISBN: 978-1-914165-35-1|

|First Published Spring 2021| 174 Pages|
|Printed in the United Kingdom|

| Book Designer: Studio Mehri |
| Cover Designer: Carolyn Shaw |

www.mehripublication.com
info@mehripublication.com

TABLE OF CONTENTS

Chapter II

The Defendants' Biographies;
More Details of the Terror Attack Plan

Chapter III

Chapter IV

Interview With Parviz Dastmalchi

"Parviz Dastmalchi's book provides chilling details of an Iranian sponsored terrorist attack by someone who was there. It's recounting of the planning, carrying-out, and eventual trial of those responsible for the 1992 assassination in a Berlin restaurant of members of a Kurdish political group is a vivid and bloody reminder of why Iran has long been considered the world's leading state sponsor of terrorism abroad. Dastmalchi's book puts faces and names to both the perpetrators and victims of terrorism and should be read by everyone who wishes to understand the truly evil nature of the Mullah's regime in Iran."

— The Honourable Senator Linda Frum, Senate of Canada

"This is a fascinating and illuminating book. It is a riveting account of a historical trial.

Justice is my profession. "Terror in the Name of God" should be read by anyone who cares about justice throughout the world."

— Dr. Pamela Milan MD, Attorney-At-Law,
Supreme Court of the United States

"Since the 1979 revolution, successive leaders of Iran's brutal theocratic regime have not only detained, tortured and murdered many thousands of their fellow citizens but also have ordered the assassination of scores of opposition politicians in exile in

Western Europe and United States.

The most nefarious attack took place in the Mykonos Restaurant in Berlin in the Fall of 1992.

"Terror in the Name of God" is the first English translation of the detailed account of the planning and execution of that bloody attack by celebrated political scholar and activist, Parviz Dastmalchi, who survived that deadly evening.

Dastmalchi meticulously lays out the evidence by which a German court traced direct responsibility back to the Iran's notorious secret ''Special Affairs Committee'' headed by the Supreme Leader Ayatollah Khamenei. "Terror in the Name of God" is a gripping read - a chilling look inside the Iranian regime, which is a brutally determined to eliminate all opposition today as in 1992."

— The Honourable Peter Kent,
Member of the Canadian House of Commons since 2008

''This English translation of Dastmalchi's gripping account of Iran's brutal IRGC attack on foreign soil is a must read. The theme remains timely since the IRGC shot down Ukraine International Airlines Flight PS752 and killed 176 innocent people on January 8, 2020.

IRGC is still not recognized as the terrorist organization it is, even as it funds and coordinates operations with Hezbollah and other globally-recognized terrorist operations. This work sheds light on many terrorist activities. ''

— The Honourable David Kilgour,
former member of the Canadian Parliament,
Senior Fellow to the Raoul Wallenberg Centre for Human Rights

"The Iranian regime of the mullahs since its inception has been engaged in the cold-blooded murder both at home and abroad of those who oppose its tyranny. This book is a chilling and detailed account of one such murderous attack in Berlin in 1992 and its legal aftermath. The wealth of detail is a timely reminder of who it is we are dealing with when we are dealing with Iran."

— David Matas, Attorney-At-Law, Member of the Order of
Canada, Senior Legal Counsel of B'nai Brith Canada, Author

"Parviz Dastmalchi's Terror in the Name of God is a riveting first-hand account of a terror plot carried out at the hands of the Islamic Republic of Iran. The targeted assassinations of four dissidents at the Mykonos restaurant in Berlin in 1992 is just one example of the countless crimes of the Islamic Republic since its inception. With the help of Avideh Motmaen-Far, Dastmalchi relays his research on this topic to authoritatively recount just one terrible night in which the regime committed murder of civilians in the name of God and against any who dissent from its ideology. The book gives readers a detailed picture of how a criminal government is able to execute terror on foreign soil along with how Germany subsequently dealt with bringing justice to the victims but eventually conceded the initiative to the terror regime that continues to wreak havoc around the world by exporting its ideology. Iran watchers, analysts of terror and totalitarianism, and those interested in learning specifically how the Islamic Republic of Iran and the Islamic Revolutionary Guard Corps operate would benefit from reading this book."

— Saghar Erica Kasrsie, Middle East advisor at U.S. House of
Representatives, Senior Iran Fellow at Security Studies Group,
Executive Director Living Water Productions

"Terror in the name of God by Parviz Dastmalchi explains brilliantly and in great detail the somber modus operandi of one the most vicious terrorist regimes in History. This celebrated scholar, who was present during the events of the infamous Mykonos Restaurant attack in Berlin, paints a dark portrait of the Iranian regime and shows how far it is willing to go to ensure the spreading of their dangerous ideology. It will not leave a single reader indifferent. This book is a step in the right direction to expose the horrors perpetrated by the extremist Iranian government and help put an end to its theocratic reign."

— The Honourable Senator Leo Housakos, Senate of Canada

Translator's Note

In *Terror in the Name of God*, Parviz Dastmalchi relives the brutal attack he and others endured at the Mykonos restaurant in Berlin, September 17, 1992. The attack left four dead, one wounded, and made a chilling statement: The world is not safe for those who oppose the regime controlling the Islamic Republic in Iran. As Mr. Dastmalchi notes in his own preface, the IRI began its campaign of global terror with an assassination in Paris in 1979, more than 40 years ago. With this translation, I echo the author when he asks, when will it end?

This account is important, vital, in so many ways.

First of all, consider the source. Writer and political scholar, Parviz Dastmalchi has spent his career fighting the IRI. He has given a voice to global Iranians, displaced by the Islamic Revolution, as well as those still suffering oppression at home. And regarding the terror attack at the Mykonos restaurant, Dastmalchi offers a primary view, a harrowing voice that could only have been earned through what he has suffered. His accounting of the events of that evening is clinical and brutal, the kind of statement that can only be made by one who was there.

The account pays respect to those who lost their lives in the attack: Dr. Mohammad Sadegh Sharafkandi, Fatah Abdoli, Homayoun Ardalan, and Nouri Dehkordi. The first three were displaced leaders of the PDKI, the Democratic Party of Iranian Kurdistan. Mr. Dehkordi was an active member of the global Iranian resistance, living in Berlin. These victims had already suffered life in exile as their homeland fell to the political tyranny of the Islamic Republic. Ultimately, the IRI demanded a punishment greater than exile. The regime's reach extended all the way to democratic Germany.

In addition to honouring the lives and contributions of the victims, and sharing the events of the attack in graphic detail, Mr. Dastmalchi goes one step further. He lays out the case against those who perpetrated the attack in a clear and concise manner. Rather than let the murderers' identities fade into anonymity, Dastmalchi gives us their history as well. He gives us a window into the investigation that followed the attack, leading us, step by step, to the trial and conviction of some (but not all) of those responsible for the events of that night.

He examines the two shooters, Abdol-Rahman Banihashemi and Abass Rhayel. Banihashemi, an experienced agent and assassin, led the hit team on the ground in Berlin and wielded the Uzi. Abass Rhayel, a young Lebanese national, was armed with a pistol and tasked with following up on the targets. Dastmalchi also gives us the background of the others involved in the plot. Youssef Amin was the lookout. Farajollah Haidar drove the getaway car. Ali Sabra purchased the car for the operation. Mohammad Atris provided the passports and travel documents that would allow their escape. Planning and logistics were provided by Kazem Darabi.

The investigation and the ensuing arrests illustrate an elaborate web connecting these men to each other, to Hezbollah, to the Islamic Revolutionary Guard Corps, and finally up to high-ranking officials in the Iranian Intelligence community and even the Supreme Leader, Ayatollah Ali Khamenei. It is impossible to overstate the importance of the facts that were revealed throughout the trial that followed.

Parviz Dastmalchi weaves together the trail of clues left in the wake of the attack, along with unprecedented testimony by former Iranian President Abolhassan Banisadr. Under threats to his life and family, Banisadr shed light on the inner working of the IRI's Special Affairs Committee and its connection to the Islamic Revolutionary Guard Corps, illustrating that any command issued from the SAC had the approval of the Supreme Leader himself. Banisadr also introduced the anonymous Witness C, now known to be Abolghasem (Farhad) Mesbahi. Mesbahi was a high-ranking member of the IRI's Intelligence and Foreign Affairs Agencies. He also testified under threat to life and limb.

Looking back on the trial, nearly 25 years later, it is important to note the lengths to which the Iranian regime went to stifle the prosecution in the German courtroom. The Iranian Consulate lobbied incessantly, to be sure that there would be no mention of the Special Affairs Committee, the IRGC, or the Islamic Republic of Iran. They had some success. What should have been completely impartial judicial proceedings were tainted by political pressure. While the trial ended with convictions, and the IRI's involvement was disclosed, the entire affair also highlighted the power wielded by the Supreme Leader.

Sadly, there are still lessons to be learned from the 1992

16 Mykonos Restaurant attack and the trial that followed.

The regime surrounding the Ayatollah has changed little in the past quarter-century, and the nations of the West still deal with Iran by employing sanctions and half-measures. The IRGC funnels money and weapons to Hezbollah, the Taliban, and other terrorist organizations with impunity. Yet Canada, and other nations, are reluctant to declare the IRGC a terrorist entity. The Quds Force, a military arm of the IRGC, has been declared a terrorist force. Yet the greater umbrella of the Revolutionary Guard is free to continue operations and even to fund Quds and other sanctioned cells.

In 2018, the Canadian Parliament passed a measure to place the IRGC on a terror watchlist. It is now 2020 and the government has yet to act on the measure.

In January of 2020, IRGC shot down Ukrainian International Airlines Flight 752, as it took off from Tehran destined for Kiev. After spending three days vehemently denying any involvement in the incident, the IRGC finally claimed responsibility, admitting that an individual mistook the commercial flight for a threat, and fired a rocket. Of the 176 passengers killed in the attack, 55 were Canadian and another 30 were permanent residents in Canada. Much like Germany feared making the regime culpable in the Mykonos attack, nations today fear calling out Iran and its IRGC's terrorist activities. They fear making a bad situation worse, never noting that the IRI is growing bolder.

Which is why it is so important to bring Parviz Dastmalchi's *Terror in the Name of God* to a wider audience. The story it tells is still so very relevant today, more than 25 years after the attack it describes.

Avideh Motmaen-Far
President of the Council of Iranian Canadians

Preface

The first victim of a series of assassinations conducted by the Islamic Republic, but outside of Iran, was Shahriar Shafigh, son to the Princess Ashraf Pahlavi and Mr. Ahmad Shafigh. Shahriar Shafigh was a high-ranking officer of the Imperial Iranian Naval Army. He was assassinated in December, 1979. Two gun shots, on a Sunday afternoon in Paris, while leaving his sister's house.

Mullah Sadegh Khalkhali, a judge assigned by Khomeini, wrote in his memoirs in the "Islam" newspaper, years later, that Shahriar Shafigh was convicted on charges of "corruption on earth" by the Islamic Revolutionary Court, and therefore condemned to death.

Mullah Sadegh Khalkhali, regarding the manner in which revolutionary Muslims should fight dissidents says, *"...for most of my colleagues, the question was how to deal with MEK* [The People's Mojahedin Organization of Iran] *... one afternoon we were coming back from Imam Khomeini's house and in the street, I saw two young boys, 15 or 16 years old, exchanging something secretly. I ordered them arrested right away to find out what was going on. I searched them myself and found a newspaper that belonged* *to MEK in their bags. I remember one of them, his name was Shariati. I shot them both dead on the spot. And I told my colleagues, 'this is how you deal with these animals.'"[1]*

There have been many victims of Muslim fundamentalists in Iran. Some of those responsible officially admitted to having been involved in killing dissidents, others were forced to make avowals. A few assassination agents confessed to their crimes while some were convicted at trial.

We all know the name of the first victim of the Islamic Republic's assassinations outside the country, Shahriar Shafigh. The last one? Not sure yet! The Mykonos trial convicted the agents with a heavy sentence and provided proof of state sponsored terrorism originating from the Islamic Republic of Iran, involving high profile religious and political figures. The Supreme Leader, Seyed Ali Khamenei, the then sitting President Hojjatoleslam Akbar Hashemi Rafsanjani, Minister of Intelligence Hojjatoleslam Ali Fallahian (superintendent of the operations), and Foreign Minister Dr. Ali Akbar Velayati (a pediatrician), all responsible for the Berlin assassination and the assassination of other dissidents outside Iran. Of course, the verdict created hysteria in the relations between Iran and the European Union. In order to re-establish and normalize the relations with Europe, the regime's senior officials pledged not to commit any assassinations in the EU and indeed, since April 10, 1997, no assassinations have been linked to the Islamic Republic of Iran. This is anti-theorematic to the Islamic Republic's claim that the assassinations were the work of some unauthorized rogue groups.

But the EU is not the entire world. The witness, Abolghasem Mesbahi, senior Official of the Intelligence Minis-

1. (Parvin Weekly, Number 0, 1381)

try and coordinator of IRI secret activities in Western Europe, testified in court, *"...as long as Ayatollah Khomeini lived, all assassinations inside and outside the country were carried out only by his direct order or agreement. After he passed away, everything was decided by Ayatollah Ali Khamenei. He created an organization named the 'Special Affairs Committee,' to decide on which assassinations were to be carried out, with he, the Supreme Leader himself, as the head of this Committee."*

The 41-year-old history of the IRI is full of atrocity and adversity, although they promised equality and fraternity. The wheel of the IRI is still turning, but perhaps it will not be long before it stops. As history didn't forget or forgive the atrocities and crimes of Nazism and Stalinism, the crimes of those promising "divine mercy" will not stay hidden either.

The past is the light of the future. To build an open society, we need to educate responsible and conscientious people. Crimes must not be forgotten and criminals must be prosecuted, so no one thinks that by being out of reach, time will erase the memories of their crimes. A person's life can never be replaced. To prevent the repetition of these horrendous events, we need to wake up people's conscience. A society's moral and ethical standards should be solid and unshakable. When individual's responsibility is reinforced by wisdom, and not its imitation, then individuals will act responsibly. We must create moral and ethical principles that are universal and do not change under any circumstances. Without such standards for all, regimes and rulers will experience the moral collapse we are witnessing in the IRI. We need to understand that without these universal moral principles, politics will become a crime and the politicians, criminals. An ethical politician wants order to

20 protect people and life. But a politician who merely plays the role of a moral politician will sacrifice people to their imaginary "divine order." Those who do evil in order to prevail good are, themselves, the most evil.

This book is dedicated to all known and unknown, popular and private, official and unofficial victims of a regime, which, in its obscenity, atrocity, adversity, and discrimination, is one of the most significant evils in Iran, and in the world.

Parviz Dastmalchi
Berlin

Chapter I

The Assassination Chronology: From the "Special Affairs Committee" to the Verdict

On the 17th of September, 1992, at around 10:50pm, an agent of the Islamic Republic of Iran (IRI) and two Lebanese citizens, members of Hezbollah, entered the Mykonos Restaurant, in the Wilmersdorf district of Berlin. The agent started shooting people in the private dining room of the restaurant with a machine gun. One of the other two men followed up by administrating the "coup de grace" to two of the victims. The third person guarded the door.

The primary targets of the Mykonos operation were Dr. Mohammad Sadegh Sharafkandi, the Secretary-General of the Democratic Party of Iranian Kurdistan PDKI, Fatah Abdoli, the PDKI's European representative, and Homayoun Ardalan, the PDKI's representative in Germany. Nourrollah Dehkordi, a friend of Dr. Sharafkandi, was also killed in the attack, and Aziz Ghaffari, the owner of the Mykonos restaurant, was wounded.

The attackers directed one of the bloodiest massacres

of foreign nationals ever to occur on German soil.

The people dining at the table when the assassination happened were:

1-.Dr. Mohammad Sadegh Sharafkandi, the Secretary-General of the PDKI;
2- Fatah Abdoli, the PDKI's European representative;
3- Homayoun Ardalan, the PDKI's representative in Germany;
4- Nouri Dehkordi, a close friend of Dr. Sharafkandi, an activist of the Democratic Left, residing in Berlin;
5- Parviz Dastmalchi;
6- Mehdi Ebrahimzadeh Esfehani;
7- Massoud Mirrashed;
8- Esfandiar Sadeghzadeh; and,
9- Aziz Ghaffari, the owner of the restaurant.

The meeting was held to allow the opposition members to become better acquainted, exchanging ideas and talking about Iran. It was Dr. Sharafkandi who had insisted on the gathering. The delegation of the Democratic Party of Iranian Kurdistan PDKI was already in Berlin to participate in the XIX Congress of Socialist International, held in Berlin from September 15 to 17, 1992.

The Mykonos attack can be traced back to the IRI's Special Affairs Committee. This committee was established by the order of the Supreme Leader of IRI, Ayatollah Ali Khamenei, following the death of the Ayatollah Khomeini in 1989. One of the committee's purposes is the suppression and physical elimination of political opposition to the Islamic Republic.[2]

---

2. Witness statement of Abolghasem Mesbahi (Witness C) on Sep. 26, 1996, Criminal System: Documents of the Mykonos Case 171

The Special Affairs Committee is an illegal organization. Its existence is not implied in Iran's Constitution, nor has it been voted on by the Islamic Consultative Assembly (Parliament in Iran). Once the decision to liquidate a political opponent is made, the Special Operations Council (shoray-é-amaliyat-é-vijeh) of the Ministry of Intelligence is in charge of implementing the decisions.

In early days of 1991, the Special Affairs Committee (komitey-é-omour-é-vijeh) decided to eliminate the delegation from the Democratic Party of Iranian Kurdistan.

The political context in which this decision was made highlights the importance the Islamic Republic of Iran placed on the success of the operation.

The Democratic Party of Iranian Kurdistan (PDKI) is the leading Kurdish political party in Iran and one of the most outspoken political groups opposing the Islamic regime. Advocating for Kurdish autonomy in administrative, legal, and educational matters, is at the core of this Political Party. Its motto is "Democracy for Iran, Autonomy for Kurdistan."[3]

The PDKI publicized the Party's proposal for Kurdish autonomy in March, 1979, immediately after the Islamic Revolution. The new revolutionary government strongly opposed the idea of Kurdish autonomy and accused the PDKI of plotting for independence instead. Khomeini, then the Supreme Leader, labeled the PDKI the "Party of Satan,"[4] and made membership of the party a crime against the IRI, therefore punishable according to law.[5] The PDKI

3. Khudmukhtari Baray-i Kurd, Dimokrasi Baray-I Iran [Autonomy for the Kurd, Democracy for Iran], AYANDIGAN (Tehran), No. 3306, (March 7, 1979)

4. [Imam's Message to the People of Kurdistan: The PDKI is The Party of Satan], ETTELA'AT (Tehran), No. 15934, August 21, 1979

5. [The Islamic Revolutionary Council Announced: Kurdish Democratic Party is Illegal], KAYHAN (Tehran), No. 10785, August 19, 1979

was forced underground, but armed confrontations between the peshmerga and government forces continued.

Dealing with the outbreak of the Iran-Iraq war in September, 1980, the Islamic Republic was forced to pay urgent attention to its northern border where the government controlled the major Kurdish cities but many rural areas remained under PDKI control. In July, 1984, the Islamic Republic managed to drive the PDKI forces across the border into Iraq. Ultimately, forcing the leaders of the PDKI out of Iran was not enough. The Islamic Republic resorted to assassination to disrupt their activities.

At the time of the Mykonos assassinations, the permanent members of the "Special Affairs Committee" were Akbar Hashemi Rafsanjani, then President; Ali Fallahian, then Minister of Intelligence; Ali Akbar Velayati, then Foreign Minister; Mohammad Reyshahri, a former Minister of Intelligence; Ayatollah Khazali, a member of the Guardian Council; Mohsen Rezai, then General Commander of the Islamic Revolutionary Guard Corps; and Reza Seifollahi, then head of the Islamic Republic of Iran's police.

But the Special Affairs Committee's decisions were only implemented if the Supreme Leader confirmed and signed the decision.

The Mykonos operation was executed under the code name "Faryad Bozorg Alavi," roughly translated, "the outcry of the Shi'ite religious leader," referring to Ayatollah Seyed Ali Khamenei, the leader of Shi'ites in the world.

The Special Affairs Committee communicated its decision to a committee gathered in the Turquoise Palace (Ghassr-é-Firouzeh) in Tehran. This committee's responsibility was to coordinate the executive plan. The Turquoise Palace Committee is under the close and direct supervision of the Supreme Leader himself. Moreover, the Turquoise

Palace Committee includes representatives from the offices of the President of the IRI, the Islamic Revolutionary Guard Corps' Commander-In-Chief, and the Intelligence and Security Minister. They prepare the executive plan in two copies, one for the Leader and one for the President. After confirmation of the plan by the Leader and the President, the order is communicated to the regime's executive organ. The plan "Faryad Bozorg Alavi," or "the outcry of the Shi'ite religious leader," was then communicated to the Minister of Intelligence and Security, Ali Fallahian.

In the summer of 1991, when Hojjatoleslam Fallahian received the assignment to eliminate the PDKI leadership, he immediately directed a person named Mohammad Hadi Hadavi Moghaddam, an agent of the IRI Ministry of Intelligence, to travel to Germany to gather information on Kurdish opposition groups and the leaders of the Democratic Party of Iranian Kurdistan PDKI.[6]

Moghadam was considered the right person for that task for several reasons. Being the CEO of the Samsam Kala Company provided him an adequate cover story. He had provided previous good services to IRI Intelligence and Security Agency (VAVAK) in the past. And he had already successfully collaborated with the Ministry in 1989, organizing the assassination of the PDKI's Dr. Abdul Ghassemlou in Vienna. Without arousing any suspicion, Moghaddam prepared a report and presented recommendations, which were then forwarded to the Special Operations Council by Fallahian.[7]

Moghaddam's information and recommendations were followed up on in June, 1992, by two high-ranking

---

6. Witness statement of Abolghasem Mesbahi (witness C) on Sep. 26, 1996.

7. Mykonos Urteil [Mykonos Judgment], Urteil des Kammergerichts Berlin vom 10. April 1997 [Judgement of the Court of Appeal of Berlin on April 10, 1997]

operatives of the IRI Ministry of Intelligence, Asghar Arshad and Ali Kamali, close friends of Fallahian. They traveled to Berlin to assess the feasibility of undertaking the assassinations in Germany.[8]

Once the practicability of undertaking the assassination in Germany was established, Fallahian put his best operative, Abdol-Rahman Banihashemi, in charge of the operation. He was familiar with Europe, and he had previously proven his suitability for the assignment, leading the hit team that had assassinated a former officer of the Imperial Iranian Air Force, Colonel Ahmad Talebi, in Geneva, Switzerland on August 10, 1987.9 Banihashemi operated the Uzi machine gun and committed the actual killings at the Mykonos restaurant.

The Islamic Republic of Iran's Ministry of Intelligence sent a team to Berlin in early September, 1992, to connect directly with the local team and plan the assassination.

The team received confirmation of the presence of the PDKI delegation, in Berlin, through a spy who had been in direct contact with the Kurdish leaders. The spy, based on information from Germany's Federal Office for the Protection of the Constitution (Bundesamt für Verfassungsschutz BfV), had even been present at the Mykonos restaurant during the assassination. The team then escaped to Iran, following a predetermined plan after the operation.

A local operative, named Kazem Darabi, was selected by the Special Affairs Unit team to provide logistics for the Mykonos assassination. Residing in Germany since

---

8. Witness statement of Abolghasem Mesbahi (witness C) on Sep. 26, 1996, [Criminal System: Documents of the Mykonos Case] 174

9. Witness statement of Abolghasem Mesbahi (witness C) on Sep. 26, and Oct. 10, 1996. [Criminal System: Documents of the Mykonos Case] 176 and 203.

Dr. Sadegh Sharafkandi

1980, Kazem Darabi, was an agent of the Islamic Republic of Iran's Ministry of Intelligence, and a veteran of the Iranian Revolutionary Guards Corps (IRGC). He was assigned to find and recruit people from Lebanese Hezbollah residing in Germany to assist in the operation. Darabi recruited four Lebanese accomplices—Youssef Mohamad El-Sayed Amin, Abbas Hossein Rhayel, Mohammad Atris, and Ataollah Ayad—known to him through their prior associations with Lebanese Shi'ite militia groups Hezbollah and Amal.

Throughout 1985 and 1986, in an IRGC training camp in Iran, these Lebanese nationals had been trained in the use of firearms, explosives and how to carry them, terror attacks, and diving.

Mohammad Atris was designated to forge passports for Abass Rhayel (the second shooter), and Amin, who guarded the restaurant's door during the operation.

Ataollah Ayad, member of the Shia Organization AMAL, was designated to plan the attack. Although, he and his plan were ultimately called off at the last minute.

Darabi was also responsible for finding a "safe house," providing the money, and other logistics for the hit team. After completing his logistics duties, Darabi himself traveled to Hamburg and Bremen to distance himself from what was about to happen.

Darabi was a member of the IRI Ministry of Intelligence and IRGC. His connection officer was, at first, Hassan Djavadi, an Iranian diplomat serving at the Iranian Embassy in Bonn. When Djavadi was deported by Germany in 1989, Morteza Gholami became Darabi's new connection officer. Even Mohammad Amani-Farani, the Iranian Consul-General in Berlin, and a high-ranking agent of the IRI Ministry of Intelligence, used Darabi to spy on the opposition.

In fact, Darabi's biggest responsibility was to gather intelligence about opposition members for the Iranian Consul in Berlin.

Dr. Sadegh Sharafkandi (middle) and Nouri Dehkordi (second from right) at the XIX Congress of Socialist International

The first time Darabi attracted the attention of the German security officials was in April, 1982. He was a board member of the Union of Islamic Students Association in Europe (UISAE), Berlin unit, along with Farhad Dianat, Sabet Guillani, and Bahman Berenjian. This Union was a cover for Hezbollah and IRGC activities. Sabet Guillani and Bahman Berenjian were both operatives for the IRI Ministry of Intelligence. When Darabi organized an attack on a student dorm that housed Iranian Opposition students, in the Western German town of Meinz, 1982, he had the help of 85 members of Hezbollah. Many people were injured and Darabi was arrested and sentenced to an eight-month imprisonment. Germany wanted to deport him but the Iranian Embassy intervened, sending a letter to the Federal Foreign Office. The German Police reconsidered expelling Darabi and others under the recommendations of the Federal Minister for Foreign Affairs (Bundesminister des Auswärtigen).

Because of such activities, Darabi was targeted by the secret services for years. A Parliamentary Committee in the Bundestag started an enquiry to determine whether the Federal Constitutional Protection Bureau, through timely intervention, could have prevented the Mykonos killings. Corresponding allegations set an alliance of deputies from the SPD and the Greens against the Bureau and its chief, then the Interior Minister Dieter Heckelmann.

In 1991, Darabi was introduced by the Iranian Consulate in Berlin. He was to represent the Islamic Republic in the International Exhibition for the Green Week festival. The Democratic Party of Iranian Kurdistan (PDKI) delegation, composed of Dr. Mohammad Sadegh Sharafkandi, the Secretary-General of the PDKI, Fatah Abdoli, the PDKI's European representative, and Homayoun Ardalan, the

PDKI's representative in Germany, were supposed to be in Berlin from September 14 to 18, 1992, because they were guests to the XIX Congress of Socialist International that was held in Berlin from September 15 to 17, 1992.

Kazem Darabi, convicted henchman in Mykonos assassination, right, Anis Naghash

They decided to meet with some of the opposition leaders and activists living in Berlin, on the evening of Thursday, September 17, 1992.

Nouri Dehkordi was assigned to coordinate this meeting, but as he was accompanying the delegation throughout the XIX Congress of Socialist International and was also translating, he asked the owner of the Mykonos Restaurant to call and invite other opposition members for the meeting.

This was the opportunity that the Ministry of Intelligence had been waiting for.

Aziz Ghaffari, the restaurant's owner who had been asked to contact prominent local Iranian dissidents and invite them to the meeting, bungled the assignment, extending an invitation for the following evening.[10]

> *"...The owner of Mykonos restaurant, Aziz Ghaffari, called more or less 15 people to invite them to the meeting that was supposed to take place on the September 17, 1992 at 8 o'clock pm in his restaurant: '...on Wednesday night, September 16, 1992, around 1:00am, Dehkordi asked the owner of the restaurant to prepare for inviting 15 people that he named. Ghaffari did what Dehkordi asked. But he invited guests not for the 17th but for the 18th. His reason for committing such a mistake was not totally clear in an acceptable way...'"*

On Thursday September 17, 1992, the Kurdish delegation arrived at the restaurant at around 8:00pm. Dehkordi was very surprised that none of the guests were there. He inquired with Ghaffari, who responded, *"You told me to invite people for Friday night at 8:00pm not Thursday!"*

Once the mix-up was revealed, hurried attempts were made to contact those absent.

> *"Dehkordi called the guests, he could not reach some of them, so only two of them could make it that night; Mehdi Ebrahimzadeh, board member of the Organization of Iranian People's Fadaian (Majority), who arrived around 10:00pm, and Parviz Dastmalchi."*

Those then present at the restaurant were the PDKI delegation, meaning Dr. Sharafkandi, Fattah Abdoli, Homayoun Ardalan, and Dehkordi, along with Parviz Dast-

---

10. The individuals invited were: Dr. Nosratollah Barati, Dr. Bahman Niroumand, Dr. Kambiz Rousta, Parviz Dastmalchi, Hamzeh Farahati, Mehdi Ebrahimzadeh Esfehani, Hassan Jafari and Masoud Mirrashed. Indictment, supra note 34, at 20.

malchi, Mehdi Ebrahimzadeh, Massoud Mirrashed (who was not invited but happened to be dinning at the restaurant), Esfandiar Sadeghzadeh (also not invited, but joined the party as he was already dinning at the restaurant), and Aziz Ghaffari, the owner of the restaurant, who was attending to the guests the whole time, but sat at the table right before the attack took place.

As talks went on, the subject of the conversation was mostly the autonomy of Iranian Kurdistan. It was almost 11:00pm. At that moment, a strong-looking, dark-haired man of medium height, wearing a hood covering his face up to his eyes, came into the private dining room in the back of the restaurant. He stood between the first and second guest at the table, took a machine gun out of a sports bag, and fired in the direction of Dr. Sharafkandi, shouting, *"Son of the whores!"* In a fraction of a second, twenty six shots of the machine gun were fired. A second man fired four fatal shots from a pistol, finishing off Sharafkandi and Ardalan. Ardalan lost consciousness when hit by the machine gun but came back for a second and moved his head. The man wielding the pistol went closer to him and fired a shot to his head. He also fired two shots to Sharafkandi's head and one to his throat. Dr. Sharafkandi was hit by twelve bullets in total, mostly to his head, throat, intestines, lungs, liver and kidney. He died on the spot.

Ardalan was hit by the machine gun to the chest, abdomen and right knee. He could have been saved if he wasn't shot another time to his head by the second killer. He died on the spot.

Abdoli who was sitting the closest to the shooter, got hit close to the heart by four bullets from the machine gun. He died on the spot.

Dehkordi was hit seven times and was transported to

the Steglitz Hospital where he died half an hour later, at 12:05am, due to internal hemorrhaging.

The owner of the restaurant was wounded in his abdomen and leg.

Four other people, Parviz Dastmalchi, Mehdi Ebrahimzadeh, Massoud Mirrashed, and Esfandiar Sadeghzadeh, got lucky.

The Uzi machine gun killer was Abdol-Rahman Banihashemi, known as Aboosharif, or Sharif. He was in command of the hit team. Abass Rhayel was the killer who fired the fatal shots with his pistol. Youssef Amin was guarding the door of the restaurant. All of them escaped the crime scene. But only Banihashemi returned to Iran. He was rewarded with an expensive Mercedes Benz 230.

The next day, the Iranian media was speculating about internal cleansing between the opposition forces or a revenge operation perpetrated by the Kurdistan Communist Party. There was no reason, motive, or evidence in support of such claims.

The next morning, Parviz Dastmalchi, one of the survivors of the attack, set up an appointment with a reporter from the Berliner Zeitung, Mr. Werner Kolhoff. He met with the reporter at 10:00am on September 18, 1992, at Café Kransler, in the same neighbourhood as the Mykonos restaurant. At 11:00am, he went to the restaurant where the attack took place the night before. More than 100 reporters from all over the world were gathered in front of the Mykonos restaurant. He explained what happened the night before and stated his belief that the Islamic Republic of Iran and its Intelligence and Security Agencies were involved in this terror attack.

The first rally in protest against the Islamic Republic of Iran, and its brutal killing of four Iranians, took place in front of the city hall building in Berlin, the day after the attack, September 18th, 1992, at 5:00pm. Almost all the different opposition groups named the regime in Tehran as responsible for the terrorist attack. A few days later, a Berlin based 'Interim Committee' for the fight against Islamic Republic terrorism was created.11

Only after the Mykonos terrorist attack, for the first time, after 15 years of ongoing terrorist attacks on Iranian dissidents outside the country, finally, was a committee named "Opposition Committee of Exiled Iranians Against Terrorism – Berlin." This led to the creation of other committees, in different cities of Germany and in Paris, all with the mandate of fighting against the Islamic Republic's state-sponsored terrorism.

This committee has been successful in shedding light on the situation, affecting public opinion in Germany regarding the Islamic Republic's acts of terrorism and, more specifically, the Mykonos Restaurant attack. In the fifth statement from the Berlin-based committee, issued on March 26, 1993, and titled, "Unite Against Terrorism To Defend Freedom Seekers Lives," it reads, "...the activities of the Opposition Committee of Exiled Iranians Against Terrorism in Berlin, Hamburg, Köln, Frankfurt, and also residents of Hannover and Darmstadt, have shown that if Iranian freedom seekers fight against terrorism in a united and focused way, they can reach members of civic society and influence public opinion."12

The Berlin Committee started widespread activity,

---

11. Book: Parts of Mykonos documents, page 17, September 92 to Avril 97, Parviz Dastmalchi, Spring 98, Berlin

12. Book: Parts of Mykonos documents, page 6o to 63, September '92 to Avril '97, Parviz Dastmalchi, Spring '98, Berlin

aiming to enlighten the public regarding Intelligence agents and the people behind the Mykonos terrorist attack. They published a document-based book, six volumes in German, about the Islamic Republic's terrorist activities. All six volumes were written and edited by Parviz Dastmalchi.

On September 22, 1992, the police found the murder weapons; a 9mm machine gun, made by IMI, with silencer, and a hand gun, a Llama Special, Model X, 65/7mm with a silencer, made in Spain. The police traced the origin of the hand gun by the serial number. It was sold by Spain to the Imperial Iranian Army during the monarchy era in 1972.

Immediately after the Mykonos attack, on September 18, the Attorney General of Germany, along with Bundeskriminalamt (BKA), the Federal Criminal Police Office of Germany, created a Mykonos Special Commission and started an investigation.

After committing the crime, the three offenders, Abdol-Rahman Banihashemi, Abass Rhayel, and Youssef Amin, escaped in the getaway car, a BMW Series 7 that was parked close to the restaurant. The two other accomplices, Mohammed and Haidar (the driver), were waiting for them at the car. Rhayel and Banihashemi exited the car at Bundesplatz U-Bahn station. A little further, at the Konstanzer straße, close to a service station, Amin and Mohammed got out of the car, and Haidar drove away alone, carrying the murder weapons inside the car.

On September 22, 2019, at around 11:15am, in an industrial area of Berlin, Wilmer Sedorov found a black sports bag with a green Sportini icon, containing weapons, hidden under a car on Cicerostraße.13

The bag contained a knitted black hat, a stripped choc-

---

13. Indictment, supra note 34, at 32.

olate-cream scarf, a leather glove, a 9mm machine gun Model Uzi with silencer, a Spanish Llama X-A automatic pistol with silencer, and three 9mm shells. These weapons were later recognized as the murder weapons used in the Mykonos operation. On October 5, 1992, Abass Rhayel's palm print was discovered on the automatic pistol.

Haidar abandoned the car in front of number 34 Cicerostraβe and hid the bag containing the murder weapons and a few pieces of clothing under a car parked on the same street. The sports bag was found by an employee of the car dealership Brolina on September 22.

The abandoned getaway car was discovered because it was blocking the driveway of the car dealership Brolina. The police did not immediately make the connection to the attack at the Mykonos restaurant, and initially, the car had simply been towed. It was not until October 7, 1992, after getting a statement from Youssef Amin, that the police searched the car. They found a spent 9mm cartridge, and a plastic bag with Amin's left index fingerprint, inside the car.

Abass Rhayel and Youssef Amin were arrested on October 4, 1992, while hiding in Amin's brother's house in Rhine, in the province of Westfalen. Amin resisted for two days before confessing the whole crime. Based on his confessions, team members Kazem Darabi Kazerouni, Mohamed Atris, and Ataollah Ayad, were arrested.

The others were able to successfully leave Germany. Arrest warrants still exist for;

   • Abdolrahman Banihashemi, leader of the operation, who escaped to Iran;
   • An individual called Mohammed, an Iranian citizen, who provided the team with the murder weapons the night before the terrorist attack;

- Farajollah Abu Haidar, a member of the Lebanese Hezbollah who lived in Osnabrück, Germany. He was the driver of the getaway car. He is currently believed to be working for the IRGC in Iran;
- Ali Sabra, Lebanese citizen, and member of Hezbollah. He was the person who purchased the getaway car BMW, licensed B-AR5503, a week before the date of the terrorist attack. He is currently believed working in Lebanon in the Hezbollah offices; and,
- An Iranian citizen, driver of a black Mercedes Benz 190 who met with Banihashemi an hour before the terrorist attack at the Mykonos restaurant. But his identity remains unknown.

The investigation was led by the Germany's chief federal prosecutor, Alexander von Stahl, and the German Bureau of Investigation. The evidence gathered through police investigation and the Intelligence Agency's reports pointed to the involvement of the Islamic Republic of Iran in the Mykonos attack.

But the German government did not seek to clarify Iran's involvement. Minister of State Bernd Schmidbauer suggested that the Special Mykonos Commission not mention *"Iran"* in their reports. According to his suggestion, the offenders should be put to trial without mention of Iran's involvement. This issue was leaked to the press, and many documents that highlighted Iran's role in this terrorist attack were published by the German media. The Federal Minister of Justice also suggested that Germany's chief federal prosecutor, Alexander von Stahl should not mention "Iran" in the indictment. On May 17, 1993, the prosecutor released the indictment and despite all the suggestions, it mentioned Kazem Darabi Kazerouni as an agent of the IRI Ministry of Intelligence and a member of the IRGC, assigned to assist in assassinating the leaders of the Democratic Party of Iranian Kurdistan during their stay in Berlin.

The indictment created turmoil between the German politicians and in the government. But all agreed that the issue should be decided by a non-partisan court. Nonetheless, Alexander von Stahl was later removed from office, because of "too many mistakes" in other cases. More likely, the German Government wanted to send a signal to others, compelling them to consider the Mykonos case only within the larger framework of German security policies.

On October 6 and 7, 1993, a few weeks before the Mykonos trial began, the IRI Intelligence Minister, Hojjatoleslam Ali Fallahian, was invited to Germany by Minister of State Bernd Schmidbauer. The visit was kept secret; however, the news was leaked by a copy of the minister's itinerary, which had been transmitted by telex to several agencies, the interior ministry and the border police, and had been intercepted by a friend of the reporter, Josef Hufelshulte. The media was outraged. Ali Fallahian, whose ministry was mentioned in the federal prosecutor's indictment, was in Germany. He had met with the Chancellor and was scheduled to meet with his Ministry counterpart, Bernd Schmidbauer, on October 7 at 11:00am.

The German's chief federal prosecutor, Alexander von Stahl wanted him arrested. But the German Government prevented his arrest under the pretext that he was an Iranian Minister and was invited by the German government, so he enjoyed political immunity. Minister of State Bernd Schmidbauer said that the meeting was purely humanitarian in nature and freedom of foreign prisoners was at the centre of his discussions with Fallahian. Regarding Mykonos, according to Schmidbauer, nothing had been discussed.

What was really exchanged between Fallahian and Schmidbauer remained a mystery for months. In the end, as Schmidbauer was facing the worst scandal of his career, the minutes of his meeting with Ali Fallahian were released:

"...F said that Iran has helped Germany a great deal. Iran pressured the Hamadi clan to release the German hostages held in Lebanon. To return the favor, Bernd Schmidbauer should help with an upcoming criminal trial in Berlin in which Iran is wrongly accused. F asked: how do you plan to stop this trial from happening?"

The consulting minister rejected the idea of interfering in the legal proceedings.

He said: "Berlin's courts are in the hands of the justice ministry and function independently of other government bodies. There is no room nor possibility for striking deals. We can try to minimize the political cost of the trial if Tehran never again conducts such an operation in Germany or Europe."

He said the same thing to the German Congress. But two years later, when the role of the IRI in the Mykonos Affair was becoming clear, under oath, as a witness in Mykonos trial, Schmidbauer admitted that when he met with Fallahian in Germany, Fallahian asked him to stop the Mykonos Trial. Schmidbauer testified that he had responded that the German Judiciary is independent and the government cannot stop the judiciary from doing its job.

"...Fallahian, the IRI Minister of Intelligence and Security, tried to convince his German counterpart to stop the Mykonos Trial, while visiting Germany on October 6 and 7, 1993. The witness to Schmidbauer, whose responsibility was

to coordinate talks between the German Intelligence agencies and those of other countries, said that Fallahian talked about the Mykonos Trial and the innocence of the suspects multiple times. Fallahian was trying to pressure Germany to stop the trial by bringing up the fact that IRI had influenced the freeing of the German hostages from the Lebanese Hamadi Clan. Fallahian also promised to do whatever he could to help to clarify this terrorist attack but he did not do anything..."

Previously, in July, 1992, during a private meeting, Schmidbauer had issued this warning to the senior Iranian officials:

"You must make me one promise. Iran cannot commit any assassinations on German soil. That would place an insurmountable hurdle in the way of our efforts on your country's behalf, especially the 'Critical Dialogue initiative.'"

The German government was still sabotaging the trial. At Schmidbauer's request, the Intelligence agencies were not forwarding information to the prosecutor and the court. The prosecutor was saying: *"I am advancing millimeter by millimeter to prove the indictment. Everywhere, I am facing sabotage."* When Minister of State Bernd Schmidbauer changed his mind and confessed the truth at the trial, that his Iranian counterpart had requested that he cover up Iran's involvement in the terrorist attack, it was not because the German government adopted a new policy, but because of the fact that he would have been guilty of making false statements under oath.

April 10, 1997, Berlin
The day of the Mykonos court ruling, Parviz Dastmalchi (right) in a
conversation with reporters

Indictment

On Nov 12, 1992, more than a month after the arrests, Parviz Dastmalchi and Mehdi Ebrahimzadeh were summoned by the office of the Federal Police in Meckenheim, to identify the suspects in the assassination of the Iranian opposition leaders, committed on September 17, 1992. After a few rounds of appearances, with suspects in different attires, Mehdi and Parviz both chose, each time, the same person from the lineup. That person turned out to be Yousef Amin.

Within minutes of having been mistaken for the killer, although he had refused to kill, Amin, enraged, asked to call his lawyer. Amin tried to strike a deal and trade information for better treatment, but because German laws prohibit bargaining, Bruno Jost did not agree. Amin spoke nonetheless. While trying not to implicate Darabi and Rhayel, minimizing the extent of their involvement, Amin confessed, giving away crucial information involving 64B Detmolder Straße, the 7 Senftenberger Ring Straße apartment, and the BMW. It was because of Amin's confession that the police recovered the getaway car, finding evidence and fingerprints, and making the connection to the murder weapons found hidden underneath another car nearby.

By mid-November, the federal prosecutor's office still believed that murders at the Mykonos could have been the work of the Kurdish armed group the PKK, despite all the evidence already in their possession.

It was around that time that Parviz was given a very important piece of information. The ballistics test had revealed that the serial number of the handgun matched that of a handgun sold by Spain in a 1972 shipment of weapons to the Iranian Royal Army. This information was leaked by a highly positioned source at BKV.

This important ballistic report was not officially released by German authorities and politicians were still trying to cover it up:

> • Machinegun, made by IMI manufacturers, Uzi model, serial number 075884, 9mm caliber, with a 32-bullet magazine
> • Handgun, made by Llama manufacturers, Model X-A, 7.65m caliber, browning, serial number 517070, 8-bullet magazine. Sold to the Iranian Imperial Army.

Given the silence of the German authorities on the ballistic report, Parviz Dastmalchi decided to release the information to the *Bild* journal (German Media), and force the hands of German officials. He named Germany instead of Spain as the supplier of the weaponry in 1972 thinking that this incrimination would goad the Germans into denying the accusation by coming forth with the truth.

On May 11, 1993, as a result of the information planted in the journal *Bild*, the federal prosecutor came forward and spoke of the true origins of the murder weapons.

More than six months after that Alexander Von Stahl had assigned Bruno Jost to the Mykonos case, Jost submitted the first draft of the indictment to the chief federal prosecutor in March, 1993. The chief federal prosecutor then alerted the ministry of justice. The order came that he should neither sign nor release the indictment before the justice ministry, the chancellery, and the foreign ministry had approved it. Alexander Von Stahl found this demand to be a violation of the independence of his office. Although his party had historically been in favor of doing business with Iran, Von Stahl refused to put any interests above the law. Nonetheless, he followed orders and sent copies of the indictment to all three offices. Two months later, there was still no word from the ministries. When the chief federal prosecutor inquired about the delay, he was told that the drafts were lost.

On May 17, 1993, frustrated by the German government, the German federal prosecutor Bruno Jost, lead investigator of the Mykonos operation, announced the indictment of the accused naming Amin, Darabi, Rhayel, Atris, and Ayad. He released the indictment to Berlin's high criminal court, requesting a trial date. The indictment, signed by Germany's chief federal prosecutor, Alexander von Stahl, stated that Darabi's assignment was to "liquidate" the leaders of the Democratic Party of Iranian Kurdistan PDKI, as part of a "persecution strategy of the Iranian Ministry of Intelligence against the Iranian opposition."[14]

One month later, the court granted the request for trial.

It was the first time since World War II that a German court would consider the crimes of a foreign government.

By releasing the indictment, Alexander Von Stahl violated too many allegiances. The Minister of Justice asked

---

14. Thomas Sancton, Iran's State of Terror, TIME, Nov. 1996 at 78

for his resignation two months later.

Amin, Darabi, and Rhayel were indicted on four counts of murder and one count of attempted murder. Atris and Ayad were indicted on four counts of aiding and abetting murder and one count of aiding and abetting an attempted murder.

from right to left: Kazem Darabi, Abbas Rhayel, Yousef Amin, (fourth person unknown) at Darabi and Ayad's dry cleaning shop

Trial

On October 28, 1993, the trial of the five Mykonos suspects opened officially at 9:00AM in the largest courtroom of its kind in Europe, Berlin's High Criminal Court. Widespread security measures were in place. The entirety of the Palace of Justice (Landgericht, Berlin) was under police and intelligence surveillance. Everywhere and everyone, in the streets around the court building, on the rooftops, pedestrians...all under police control. To enter the building and the court room, people were thoroughly inspected and needed to show a valid ID or passport.

A horde of journalists from all over the world were present inside and outside of the court, reporting and broadcasting every second of the trial to the world. Inside the courtroom, sitting at the bench, were the five board members of the court, a reserve judge, and the court secretary. Chief Judge Frithjof Kubsch presided over the proceedings. A team of six Arab and Persian translators were also present and placed side by side. They swore an oath to translate accurately and truthfully.

On the right, protected by bulletproof glass cages, were the defendants Kazem Darabi and Abbass Rhayel. Yousef

Amin, Mohamad Atris, and Ataollah Ayad were placed on the left. They were all well-groomed and smiling. They did not seem to be taking the trial very seriously, perhaps because they thought that with the Islamic Republic's help and intervention, they were going to be freed and that money and fame were awaiting them.

In Germany, Judges are not political appointees. Because of this, they are less vulnerable to pressure and outside influence. The Mykonos trial had no jury. These five judges studied the case very closely for weeks, asking their own questions and making their own judgments. The trial would not be decided based on misunderstood or poorly assessed facts.

The counsels for the accused, and especially Kazem Darabi's counselor, tried very hard to sabotage the trial's timing. They entered a series of motions asking to postpone the trial, under the pretext that the prosecution had not surrendered all the evidence. This demand was rejected because it didn't correspond to the reality. Then they claimed that the dossiers had been given to the counselors too late and they did not have enough time to fully study the case. This demand was rejected also by the court because it was not true. Then Darabi's attorney demanded that the court must not have read the Prosecutor's indictment, because it was founded on faulty charges. This request was also rejected because it was obviously unreasonable. Darabi's attorney's final rogation was, "not to read the section of the Prosecutor's indictment that involves the Islamic Republic of Iran's role in the Mykonos Restaurant terrorist attack." It was clear that this request would not be granted by Judge Kubsch, because it went against normal court proceedings. At last the defendants' attorneys argued that the trial could not begin until the court had heard from Bernd Schmidbauer. The judges finally agreed to subpoena Germany's Chief of Intelligence. But the trial did not stop for a single witness.

Each time the Judge called on Bruno Jost to read the indictment, the defense attorneys entered a new motion trying to delay the trial's opening.

Parviz Dastmalchi had to stay out of the courtroom, because his position as a major eye-witness would have been compromised by his presence in the courtroom before testifying. Toward the end of the first day, the Chief Judge Kubsch rejected all motions and called on Jost to begin by reading the indictment.

The day before the trial started, Lebanese Hezbollah took Amin's family hostage to force him to change his confession. According to Amin's first confession, Kazem Darabi had been the leader of the attack assigned by the government of the IRI and its Intelligence Ministry. Repeating these confessions and charges, in court, by one of the suspects, would have been immediately damaging to the IRI. So, by taking Amin's family hostage in Lebanon and threatening to kill them, the IRI hoped to force him to change his confessions. Amin complied.

The first witness, Yousef Amin, as expected, started by denying all confessions and his "milles et une nuit" tale began:

> *"Everything I have said before has been a lie, but today I am going to tell the truth. I have been saving it for you, Judge!"*

When he was asked why he lied before, he claimed he had confessed under torture.

The second day, returning to the stand, Amin accused

his attorney of incompetence and of spying for the intelligence services. He refused to speak as long as his attorney remained present. His attorney, Luther Bunegart, resigned immediately. A new attorney was assigned, but Amin's behaviour changed little. He claimed that his confessions were wrongly translated, that the translator was a Mossad spy, or that the police and the prosecutor had written the words themselves and that they were all wrong because he spoke a different dialect of Arabic.

After five days of witness testimony, Amin calmed down when he realized he could not undo his previous confessions.

It was clear that no one would believe what Amin was claiming because it was he who had pointed out the terrorists' safe house to the police. And it was in that house that they had found the terrorist's fingerprints that led to some of the arrests. Indeed, all the police and prosecutor's investigations were proving Amin's confessions. Of course, Amin's claims and denials made the trial process longer because the court had to then subpoena the police investigator, the investigating judge, the prosecutor, the prison guard, the translator, and many other witnesses to testify.

Under the pressure of the IRI, all the Lebanese witnesses, except two of them who had already confessed and given away information about the IRI's involvement, started to deny what they had said before the trial, creating new narratives, full of contradictions. This game-playing discredited all of the Lebanese witnesses, because the evidence contradicted their claims.

This amnesia pandemic seemed to afflict all the witnesses. When they couldn't blame their memory, they blamed the translators. A Lebanese witness who had previously testified to having known Amin all his life, and to travelling with him to Iran to receive combat training, suddenly changed his mind and said that his vision had failed him before, that Amin was not the person he had thought. When pressed by the judge Kubsch, the witness begged to be dismissed because he was instructed to forget everything, otherwise he might have a car accident.

When the testimonies of the defense witnesses started, the police had spotted a witness entering the car of Oscar Brestrich, a reporter for Iran's official News agency, IRNA. When Judge Kubsch pressed the witness on how he got home after his testimony, the witness pointed out the reporter and said that the reporter was teaching him how to behave on the stand. Then he remained silent and refused to answer any more questions.

Judge Kubsch called Oscar Brestrich to the stand and asked him who his editor was. Brestrich answered that he

Abdol-Rahman Banihashemi in Sweden
on the mission to assassinate a Saudi diplomat

did not have an editor and only reported to Iran's Embassy in Bonn. When asked why he was in touch with the witnesses, he responded that he was preparing them for questioning.

Judge Kubsch found the reporter's explanations very odd and unusual. He decided to revoke Brestrich's press credentials, as reporters do not usually report to an embassy, and do not coach witnesses. Brestrich was not allowed to return to the trial.

The Austrian chief investigator in the 1989 assassination of Abdolrahman Ghassemlou in Vienna flew to Berlin to testify at the court. The investigator told the court,

"Iran's rulers have been pursuing a covert policy to annihilate the Kurdish leadership. That much is clear to me. We did our job, investigated the case fully and thoroughly. We traced the killers and found those responsible. The problem wasn't with us, the police or the investigators. It was with our politicians, who set the guilty free."

The Court was working twice a week, on Thursdays and Fridays. Everything was translated in Persian and Ar-

Abdol-Rahman Banihashemi, the main assassin

abic. Darabi, so certain that he would be freed through IRI intervention and return to Iran a hero, was insulting everybody with his vulgarity–from the presiding judge Kubsch to the witnesses, journalists, and the court's audience– and laughing in their faces

Darabi and Rhayel were called to the stand but they refused to answer any questions.

On January 16, 1994, Aziz Ghaffari, the owner of the restaurant, was called by the court to the witness stand. Rumours of his betrayal were travelling around, as a report from the Federal Office for the Protection of the Constitution (Bundesamt Für Verfassungschutz BfV) to the Department of Homeland Security indicated that Fallahian's agent was present at the restaurant on the night of the attack and had been in direct contact with the board members of the DPKI.

After three days of testimony, the court deadlocked over Aziz Ghaffari's innocence or guilt. The witness was finally dismissed.

The Federal Police investigations, the prosecutor's investigations, witnesses' statements, confidential intelligence agencies' reports, they all provided evidence pointing to the Islamic Republic's highest-ranking leaders and the IRI's Intelligence and Security Agency having a leadership role in the Mykonos assassination.

After the terrorist attack in Berlin took place, the Federal Police created a "Special Investigation Commission." The November 2, and November 13, 1992 reports issued by this commission illustrate the level of involvement the IRI Intelligence Agencies had in these murders.

A report from the Federal Office for the Protection of the Constitution (Bundesamt Für Verfassungschutz BfV) to the Department of Homeland Security introduced the prime suspect Kazem Darabi as a member of the IRI's

Intelligence and Security Agency and the IRGC, and stated that he had been working as an operative for both of these organizations in Germany. The Federal Office for the Protection of the Constitution issued another report, to the General Attorney, on December 19, 1995, indicating:

"A department of the Ministry of Information was directly involved in the assassination of the Kurdish leaders on September 17, 1992 in Berlin. This department, which is responsible for assassinations and is known as the 'special operations unit,' has been for some time hounding the members of the PDKI. A team from this department, for example, was responsible for the 1989 Ghassemlou assassination. The Ministry of Intelligence sent an assassination team to Berlin from Tehran at the beginning of September. The team met with local agents, to research and plan the assassination. The team used a Ministry of Intelligence source to concretely establish when and where the leadership of the PDKI was going to meet. This source – based on the BfV's information – was in the restaurant during the assassination. After the assassination the team left Berlin for Iran using a carefully set plan."

Witness C, Abolghasem Mesbahi (Picture courtesy of A. Mesbahi)

Victims of the Berlin Assassination
Above: Dr. Sadegh Sharafkandi (left) Nouri Dehkordi (right)
Bottom: Homayoun Ardalan (left) Fatah Abdoli(right)

The second confidential report from the Federal Office for the Protection of the Constitution (Bundesamt Für Verfassungschutz BfV), was from "Iran's Work Group." This group had been responsible for preparing a report about the Iranian Ministry of Intelligence's activities in Germany.[15]

In this report, regarding the Mykonos terror attack, we can read: *"News from a valuable trusted source that should be kept anonymous allows this conclusion, that the murder of the Kurdish leaders had been conducted by the "base" under the code name "Great Alavi."*

"Base" meant the Iranian Embassy in Bonn. The witness Abolghasem Mesbahi, Witness C, testified in court that the code name "Faryad Bozorg Alavi" represented "the outcry of the Shi'ite religious leader."

---

15. Confidential report dated June 29, 1993

This report also indicated that Fallahian's agent was present at the restaurant on the night of the attack and had been in direct contact with the board members of the DPKI. Based on this and also on previous reports, the court subpoenaed a few high-ranking members of the German Intelligence Agency to testify. Among them were Minister of State Bernd Schmidbauer, the coordinator of several different German Intelligence Agencies. He testified under oath that Ali Fallahian came to Germany to see him and asked him to stop the Mykonos Trial. He also attested that he had responded that the Judiciary in Germany is independent, and that he, Bernd Schmidbauer, could not intervene.

The judge also issued a subpoena for Klaus Grünewald, Middle East director at the (Bundesamt Für Verfassungschutz) BfV, and the signatory of the report from December 19, 1995. He testified under oath that he had been invited by a friend at another agency to study their investigations regarding the Mykonos terror attack. He attested that their intelligence matched Germany's investigations, and was complementary to it. He said based on this report, there was no doubt about the IRI's involvement.

After these reports and documents were released, chief prosecutor Bruno Jost was convinced of Iran's complicity in the assassinations. He declared that the Attorney General's Office was seeking to issue an international arrest warrant for Ali Fallahian, the Iranian Minister of Intelligence.

Fearing the eventuality of Germany issuing the warrant against Fallahian, the IRI started calling the Attorney General *"a fascist."* Vellayati, the IRI's Foreign Affairs Minister, stated in an interview that, *"What the Attorney General in Germany says is not important. What is important is that the German Government would never allow its Attorney General to arrest an Iranian Minister."*

The BfV document paved the way for Bruno Jost to implicate the masterminds behind the attack. A week later, on March 14, 1996, Chief Federal Prosecutor Kay Nehm took the unprecedented step of issuing an international arrest warrant for Fallahian. This arrest warrant exceeded Iranian exiles' wildest dreams.

The arrest warrant directly involved the IRI because Fallahian was a Minister of President Ali Akbar Rafsanjani's administration. In this way, the Mykonos trial made a huge step forward.

Investigations were going forward and witnesses were subpoenaed one after another. The defendants' attorneys were subpoenaing witnesses to attest in favor of the defendants as well. The trial was going to be adjourned and the court would render its final decision. Chief Judge Kubsch asked Bruno Jost to set an end date for the trial. The end of trial date was set to be June 25, 1996. The Attorney General and the defense attorneys were asked to prepare their closing arguments. But, right after the judge made these announcements, the IRI Foreign Ministry sent a fax to Minister of State Bernd Schmidbauer, indicating that Iran would allow them to question two new witnesses who reside in Iran, Bahram Berenjian and Mahmoud Nourara. Their goal was clear. They wanted to delay the reading of the closing arguments and therefore the verdict. It was clear that the Attorney General was going to place primary responsibility for the Mykonos terror attack on the IRI. It should be mentioned that the Attorney General and the court had wanted to question those two witnesses for the past three years, but Iran had never agreed. The judge conceded, despite the objections of the prosecutor and the victims' attorneys. The closing was postponed until after the two witnesses could be interrogated in Tehran.

A few people flew to Iran to interrogate the witnesses. Despite multiple requests, Iran did not allow the witnesses to come to the court in Berlin to testify, and ultimately only one of the two, Bahram Berenjian, was brought to the German Embassy in Tehran for questioning.

Bruno Jost, the German Federal Prosecutor

On April 20, 1996, Mr. Banisadr, former President of the IRI came to Berlin to speak at an event. Around that time, he was interviewed about terror attacks sponsored by the Islamic Republic of Iran. The German Federal Prosecutor Bruno Jost invited Mr. Banisadr to the Prosecutor's Office and asked him to share with them his knowledge regarding the Mykonos terror attack. Postponing the end date of the trial did not play in the Islamic Republic's favor. Almost two weeks after the closing date was postponed, a news story was released on Banisadr's News website. It named Abdol-Rahman Banihashemi, an agent of Iran's Ministry of Intelligence, as the terrorist who wielded the machine gun in the attack.

Abdol-Rahman Banihashemi, after committing the crime in Berlin, escaped to Iran through Turkey. This news was translated and released to the Prosecutor and the court.

Hans Ehrig, the lead attorney for the victims, asked the court to invite Mr. Banisadr to testify. Two days before Banisadr's testimony, news spread that the IRI had sent a team of five from Iran, and a team of three from Sweden, to assassinate Mr. Banisadr.

Whether this was based in fact or not is hard to know. The truth is that the IRI was trying to prevent Banisadr from testifying by frightening him. But Banisadr testified nonetheless. He told the court that the IRI Intelligence agents woke up his brother in the middle of the night, before his testimony, and said: "Warn your brother that if he goes to Berlin and testifies, we will kill him." The truth is that the regime had been trying to assassinate Mr. Banisadr since 1981. Therefore, the threat was nothing new.

Mr. Banisadr came to testify at the Mykonos trial, under heavy security measures, on August 22 and 23, 1996.

Banisadr's testimony is very important from three different angles. First, because he was the IRI's first President. Second, he was Khomeini's friend, supporter, and a member of the Revolutionary Council. And third, because

President Akbar Hashemi Rafsanjani
member of the SAC involved in Mykonos assassination

of his past position, he knew the "modus operandi" within the Islamic Republic. But despite all of that, if Banisadr had not introduced the Witness C, who added all of the detail about assassinations abroad, his own testimony would have been worthless.

Foreign Minister Ali Akbar Velayati
member of the SAC involved in the Mykonos Assassination

آخوند فلاحیان - ۱۸ تیر ۹۶

Intelligence Minister Ali Fallahian, convicted in Mykonos trial, his arrest warrant was issued by German prosecutor in May 1996

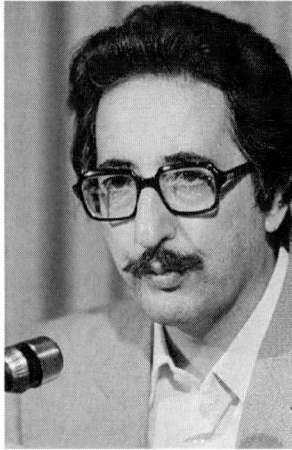

Former Iranian President
Abolhassan Banisadr's Testimony

Banisadr described, for the court, the role played by the IRI's Special Affairs Committee, in the commissioning and oversight of political assassinations. He asserted that the recommendation to assassinate an opposition figure is usually first made by the Committee and then carried out with the consent of both Khamenei and Rafsanjani. Thus, he concluded, *"The person who ordered this attack, under the current Iranian constitution and under Islamic law, can be none other than Khamenei himself."*

According to Banisadr's testimony, while Khomeini was alive, Khomeini alone could decide to order the elimination of a political opponent of the Islamic Republic. After Khomeini's death, Khamenei established the "Special Affairs Committee," in 1989, to make decisions on important matters of state. Once the committee's recommendation was approved by Khamenei (Supreme Leader), an individual committee member would be charged with implementing the decision, along with assistance from the

Ministry of Intelligence's 'Special Operations Council' at the Firouzeh (Turquoise) Palace in Tehran. The council's operational commanders received written orders, signed by the Supreme Leader, authorizing an assassination.

This Committee would send the executive plan in two copies, one for the Supreme Leader and one for the President, to get confirmation for execution by one of the Intelligence-Security units. For example, the Mykonos plan was given to the Minister of Intelligence, Ali Fallahian.

According to Banisadr's testimony, from the beginning to the end, a total of sixteen different organizations and units are involved in a planned terror attack on Iranian dissidents; from the state sponsored television, to the Iranian Ministry of Intelligence, to the Aviation Companies.

Mr. Banisadr also testified that the leader of the terrorists during the Mykonos restaurant attack was Abdolsharif Banihashemi (corrected later: Abdol-Rahman Banihashemi). According to Banisadr, this individual is now a representative of Ali Fallahian in the Ministry of Interior. He had been rewarded with the latest model of a Mercedes Benz 230 upon his arrival in Tehran, having successfully executed the Mykonos operation.

Banisadr's testimony created a lot of brawl. Iran's rulers started attacking the Mykonos Trial and the German Government once again. They pushed their discontent so far as to send Germany an extradition request for Banisadr, accusing him of airplane hijacking.

The court asked Banisadr to present his sources. Banisadr mentioned three different sources although he could not reveal their names. He said that one of his sources was a high-ranking intelligence officer who had recently defected. So, for the sake of clarity, the court called them Witnesses A, B, and C.

Witness A's testimony was based on information from supporters who were working in Iran, in various IRI organizations, and who, for obvious reasons, had to remain anonymous. Witness B's testimony was legally worthless, and the Prosecutor did not include it in the final indictment. Witness C, on the other hand, was the most important and trusted source. A few days later, Mr. Banisadr declared that witness C was ready to testify in court.

FOCUS magazine's reporter, Josef Hufelschulte was able to contact Witness C a few days later. He confirmed Banisadr's declaration, but said that because of the danger threatening him and his family in Iran, he could not testify. But Mr. Banisadr and Mr. Jost contacted Witness C and persuaded him to testify, in spite of the threats.

Witness C testified in court, during the second week of October, 1996, under heavy security measures and behind closed doors. No journalist nor audience were allowed inside the courtroom. No one was allowed to photograph Witness C. He was referred to only as "Witness C." The President of the Court reminded all those present at trial that according to German Judiciary laws, no one was allowed to repeat what has been said at the court. The atmosphere surrounding the proceedings was stressful. Witness C testified over the course of two days. In an interview, the prosecutor praised Witness C's testimony as "unique and decisive." This made the victim's and the survivor's attor-neys extremely happy.

The Iranian regime, reeling from the ground-breaking testimony, denied everything and declared that Witness C was an agent of the CIA and MOSSAD. In order to discredit Witness C, the Iranian rulers created a lengthy thirty-three page 'secret dossier' about him and sent it to the German Embassy in November, 1996. According to this file, Wit-

Abolghasem Mesbahi, Witness C

ness C had not been employed by the IRI since 1984. The IRI was portraying the witness as a charlatan, crook, and professional liar who had to flee Iran after having struggled to pay back his debt.

The court asked for time to translate this dossier and consider the content. In the meantime, the identity of Witness C came to light. He was 40-year-old Farhad (Abolghasem) Mesbahi.

Also, President Rafsanjani was threatening to release a secret file on Germany and to file a complaint against Siemens AG for not fulfilling their contracts with Iran. He accused the Germans of being manipulated by Americans and Israelis. He stated they would miss out on a contract worth twenty-five billion dollars if they did not put an end to the 'Mykonos mockery.'

Germany's Ambassador was summoned and warned that his administration would be held responsible for the German federal prosecutor's accusations against Iran's leadership. Some angry protesters even gathered in front of the German Embassy and threatened to do what they had done previously to the American Embassy. The IRGC pushed their discontent so far as to raid the German cultural attaché's residence, during a dinner in honour of several prominent Iranian writers and intellectuals. They rounded up the guests, took films of the alcoholic beverages, and charged them with 'illegal contact with enemies.' The IRGC also resorted to brutality against German citizens residing in Iran. One of them was charged with rape and found himself on death row. Even an Iranian writer, Faraj Sarekouhi, on his way to visit his family in Germany, was kidnapped by the IRGC. The Iranian authorities expedited another individual to Germany, using the writer's passport and visa. This individual X arrived in Bonn, presenting himself as the Iranian writer. Of course, the real Faraj Sarekouhi never showed up to his family waiting for him at the airport. The Iranian authorities then claimed that Faraj Sarekouhi must have been kidnapped by the German authorities.

Despite all these threats the court's work continued.

Witness C was summoned again to testify on February 6 and 7, 1997. This time in open court, because his identity was known. But still, no one had a picture of him. For the sake of security, he did not face the audience in the court, and no one was allowed to take his picture. The prosecutor, Bruno Jost, presented the following documents to the court, proving that, contrary to the IRI's claim, when Witness C had fled Iran, he was still employed by the IRI's Inter-Services Intelligence and the Foreign Affairs Ministry:

- Copies of his passports showed that he had a diplomatic passport (Blue), a government passport (Green) and a personal one. He had used all three passports for visa;
- Hotel documents showed that, while residing in different

hotels from 1984 to 1990, the passport numbers of the diplomatic passport and government passport had been used;
• German, French, and American politicians who had met with Mr. Mesbahi confirmed that during the 1987-1988 negotiations, he had been the IRI's representative with full authority to negotiate the hostage situation in Lebanon;
• A cheque that was returned by the bank, relating to when he left Iran and when the IRI had blocked his assets and belongings; and,
• Mr. Mesbahi had accompanied Mr. Rafsanjani to the Republic of Georgia in 1993, to negotiate with President Eduard Shevardnadze. The Prosecutor presented to the court pictures and video of that meeting, in which Mesbahi is at Rafsanjani's right-hand side.

So, the IRI's apocryphal dossier against Mesbahi was dismissed and the accuracy of Mesbahi's testimony was approved by the court. And again, the German media wrote that it was unprecedented in history, that the government of one country *"creates a file full of lies and presents it to the government of another country's judiciary."* They wrote that Iran's rulers were now standing *"totally naked"* in front of the Mykonos trial.

It is indeed unbelievable that the rulers of Iran had not foreseen that the German Prosecutor would be able to find evidence against their lies, and that Mesbahi would easily lead them to that proof. The Islamic Republic of Iran, fearing the consequences of this disastrous act near the end of the trial, started once again threatening the federal prosecutors, judges, witnesses, and the defense attorneys of the survivors and the victims. They dubbed the Federal Prosecutor the *"Zionists' Valet,"* and the trial, *"Advertising agencies of the great Satan."* They called upon the Democratic Party of

Iranian Kurdistan to withdraw their complaint, and in exchange, the Kurdish prisoners would be freed. Otherwise, the IRI would kill them all. Little did they know, that the PDKI's withdrawal of complaint would not change anything, because the other side of the conflict was the German Federal Prosecutor. The IRI's rulers were worried about the final indictment and they tried very hard to convince Bruno Jost not to mention Iranian high-ranking rulers. They did not even deny having committed the Mykonos crime, they were just asking not to be mentioned in the indictment. And that request was a confession in itself.

On February 14, 1997, the Mykonos trial's closing procedure began. The court levied charges against Aziz Ghaffari. Bruno Jost read his closing arguments. The reading took three days. As expected, the prosecutor pointed to the highest-ranking members of the IRI, and the Supreme Leader himself, naming them primarily responsible for the Mykonos restaurant assassination. The prosecutor acknowledged that the Mykonos Trial and Witness C's testimony allowed them to have a glimpse inside the huge assassination organization within the IRI's governing system. For Bruno Jost, there was absolutely no doubt that those responsible for this terrorist attack were sitting somewhere in the "Special Affairs Committee" in Tehran. He also mentioned in the indictment, the multiple unsuccessful attempts and efforts of both the IRI and the German Government, who tried to:

• Force him not to mention IRI anywhere in the Mykonos Trial;
• Force him to only condemn and sentence people who were physically involved in the terror attack;

• Sabotage the trial;

• Change the general opinion about the IRI's involvement by swaying the police and security forces in Germany to believe that this terror attack was the result of conflicts within Democratic Party of Iranian Kurdistan or conflicts between other Iranian Opposition groups, despite a lack of any evidence to that fact; and,

• Threaten witnesses with death, to pressure them through their families, or to offer them money, all in an effort to silence them or make them change their statements.

Also, when the German Intelligence agents were subpoenaed to testify in court, they mostly avoided the whole truth under the pretext that *"they are very limited in what they can share and testify."*

The Prosecutor said that the sum of all these conditions and situations made his job very difficult, and that he progressed millimeter by millimeter. Plus, because of threats to his own life, he was under the close watch of the Federal Police.

The survivors and the victims' attorneys, after having confirmed the Prosecutor's closing statement, also named the Supreme Leader and high-ranking officials of the IRI responsible for the terrorist attack at the Mykonos Restaurant.

The closing arguments of Attorney Otto Schily, Sharafkandi's case attorney follow:

"...These men did not know their victims, nor did they harbour any personal enmity toward them. There is but one possibility for their motive: they killed because their masters in Tehran ordered them to do so. The assassination of Dr. Sharafkandi and his colleagues did not once move Iran to inquire why the lives of its citizens were not better protected when they were in Germany for an International conference, nor have there been any words of regret or

sympathy sounded by Iran in response to this crime. The regime never once took any steps to investigate. Nor has Iran shown any desire to cooperate with the investigation. To the contrary, Iran's regime only moved into action when the accused were arrested and tried its best to prevent them from standing trial. The mask fell off Tehran's face when it tried to intervene on behalf of the accused. That alone is an admission of culpability.

"We cannot allow the hubbub in Tehran to disturb our peace, because only in peace can the judges arrive at their decision. The question is not only who committed these crimes. Names must be named, even those of the people who have evaded arrest and are not standing trial here. This will surely have political consequences for German-Iranian relations. That's for the politicians to worry about. The court must tell the truth in all its clarity and disregard all other concerns. The terrorism conducted by Iran is one of the most hateful forms of organized crime. Any concession to it is a sign of weakness on our part, and a great disrespect to our lawful way of life, and could only serve to embolden Tehran. The people of Germany want to have friendly relations with the people of Iran. We regard their culture and civilization highly. But the universality of human rights, our right to live according to our own lawful order, demands that we take the strongest stance against acts of terror.

"For much too long, European governments have watched Iran's violent behaviour. A regime that touts terror and even commands it must not be the recipient of our loans or red-carpet receptions. After all Iran has done to stonewall this trial, in these last days we hear vulgar calls and unfounded accusations coming from them again. Our federal prosecutors have been threatened with death. I fear such threats will only get louder in the days before the judgment. Which is why I must emphasize once more: we are indebted to the federal prosecutor. This gratitude is most heartfelt es-

pecially by the victims' families. If there are those in Tehran who think it is possible to make threats against our prosecutor without impunity, they must know that doing so is a declaration of war against all of Germany. Soon the judges will issue their final judgment in the name of the people of Germany.

"I am confident their judgment will be a fair one. This is my greatest hope because we all have a shared duty. All of us citizens, men and women, and even those who are our guests, must live in safety and without fear."

The final statement was made by attorney Hans Ehrig. He had never missed a day during the 3 and a half years of the trial:

"Ladies and gentlemen, the attack was ordered! How do we know this? We know this because since the fall of the Soviet Union and the United States' establishment of a no-fly zone over northern Iraq, Iran has quashed its own Kurds' demands for autonomy more vehemently than ever before. There are also ideological reasons at work here. As one of our experts quoted, Ayatollah Khomeini had demanded that, "the Kurds must choose between being Muslims following the orders of Allah and their Kurdish nationalism." Further evidence? The assassination of Abdolrahman Ghassemlou in 1989 in Vienna. Or the statement by Minister Ali Fallahian on Iranian television days prior to the assassinations, in which he targets the Democratic Party of Kurdistan as one of the ministry's top priorities, and reminds the viewer of past blows dealt to the party, and those that are yet to happen. Or the meeting between Mr. Schmidbauer and Minister Ali Fallahian prior to the start of this trial, and Iran's Foreign Minister's repeated request for the better treatment of the prisoners. Not just for Kazem Darabi, the only Iranian citizen in custody, but also for the other four accused,

who are not Iranians. Iran has extended citizenship to the Lebanese men here, in the same way that Stalin declared the Soviet Union the paternal home of all the downtrodden. Or in his testimony, Yousef Amin quotes Abbas Rhayel as having said, 'If you ever get arrested, do not worry! Iran is behind us.' Or the statement of Mr. Jalal Talebani, the Iraqi Kurdish leader, about the intelligence his men had gathered, on a plan to assassinate the main victim in this case, Dr. Sharafkandi. Or the source of the weapons used in the assassination, which the ballistic studies proved to have been Iranian in origin. Or the source of the silencers, also Iranian. Or the fact that two Iranians were involved in this operation. And that the main gunman shouted an expletive at the victims, not to mention the myriad evidence provided by German intelligence and then the damning testimony of Witness C, former President Banisadr, and others who have shown the court how the regime in Tehran has deemed this operation a victory."

With closing statements made, the trial was adjourned and the fate of the Mykonos attack was left in the board of judges' hands.

No one was really paying attention to the severity of the offenders' sentences, it was enough that they were proven guilty of their crime. No one was concerned with the mentioning of the IRI's Ministry of Intelligence, because its involvement was quite clear. The only question that remained was whether or not Iran's high-ranking officials were going to be named as responsible for the Mykonos terror attack. The rulers in Iran were not even concerned with proving their innocence. They said that if they were implicated in this attack, it would be an insult to "religious sacred beliefs" and to the "world Muslim population," so they would not remain silent.

The Judgment

The trial came to an end. It lasted almost four years, held 246 sessions, heard 176 witnesses, and cost three million dollars. The Berlin Court of Appeal issued its final judgment on April 10, 1997.

At dawn on that day, the streets leading to the court were blocked and placed under heavy security measures. Iranians from all over Europe were circulating at the four corners of the intersection surrounding the court.

For his role in killing four people, Kazem Darabi was convicted and sentenced to life imprisonment. The judgment noted: "Darabi... organized the killings for the Iranian secret services. He knew the goal and willingly participated in the destruction of four human lives."[16]

Abbas Hossein Rhayel was also convicted and sentenced to life in prison. The court found Rhayel guilty of firing at least some of the fatal shots.[17]

Youssef Mohamad El-Sayed Amin was found guilty as an accessory to the four murders and was sentenced to

---

16. Mykonos Judgment, supra note 27, at 385
17. Mykonos Judgment, supra note 27, at 375

eleven years in prison.[18]

Mohammad Atris was also convicted of being an accessory to the murders and was sentenced to five years and three months.[19]

Ataollah Ayad was acquitted and released after being remanded in custody pending trial for four years.[20]

The presiding Judge Frithjof Kubsch continued:

> *"It was clear from the beginning that this would be a long trial. And so, it was. The defendants exercised their right not to speak so they added to the court the burden to work even harder. There were many other unanticipated complications that prolonged the trial. The proceedings had to be translated into at least two languages at all times. Some witnesses were presented too late or at times, they were only available in other parts of the world...*
>
> *"...the media says that it is Iran that is on trial in this court. This is not true. We do not try anyone 'in absentia.' When a defendant had a toothache, we canceled the trial session because our court could not convene in the absence of a defendant. We do not try anyone that cannot be present. So, 'governmental terrorism' has never been on trial in this court..."* But he emphasized that the court had a responsibility to uncover the reasons and motives for the crime. He continued: *"The accused here are not the true culprits of this crime...the orders for the crime that took place on September 17, 1992, in Berlin, came from Iran's Supreme Leader."*

The lengthy 395-page decision of the court made it clear that trial had proved *"Iran's political leadership or-*

---

18. Mykonos Judgment, supra note 27, at 386

19. Mykonos Judgment, supra note 27, at 390

20. Mykonos Judgment, supra note 27, at 3-4

dered the crime."[21] While Judge Kubsch did not name
Iranian officials, he noted that witness testimony and other
evidence showed that Iran's *"Special Affairs Committee"*
had ordered the murders, and that the Supreme Leader,
President, Foreign Minister, and Intelligence Minister were
all active members of that committee.

> *"...The previous statements make it clear, that the assas-*
> *sination of the leaders of the DPK-I (PDKI) under Dr.*
> *Sharafkandi, was neither the act of individuals, nor caused*
> *by conflicts within the opposition groups themselves. Rath-*
> *er, the assassination is the result of the work of the rulers in*
> *Iran. The accused had neither a personal relationship with*
> *the victims nor any other interest that would lead to an inde-*
> *pendent resolution to plan such an act. Even Darabi would,*
> *due to his intelligence connections and his subordination of*
> *the political interests of the regime, not plan an assassina-*
> *tion without an appropriate order, and because of logistical*
> *reasons, he would not even have been able to carry one out*
> *without outside help. The evidence makes it clear that the*
> *Iranian rulers not only approve of assassinations abroad*
> *and that they honor and reward the assassins; but that they*
> *themselves plan these kinds of assassinations against peo-*
> *ple who, for purely political reasons, become undesirable.*
> *For the sake of preserving their power, they are willing to*
> *liquidate their political opponents."*[22]

For the first time, an act of terrorism perpetrated by
the Islamic Republic, outside its borders, went through an
entire judicial process. And the Islamic Republic of Iran's
highest-ranking officials were named the real culprits be-

The Assassination Chronology

21. CNN Worldview: Germany Isolates Iran After Accusing Leaders of Killings
(CNN television broadcast, Apr. 10, 1997)

22. Mykonos Judgment, supra note 27, at 368-70

hind this heinous act. The political leaders of Iran gave the order for the murders. Those who issued the orders and pulled the strings were Iranian state functionaries.[23]

".... the roots of this terror attack trace back to the relations constructed after the Islamic Republic in Iran came to power. The Kurd's push for autonomy, under the leadership of the Democratic Party of Iranian Kurdistan, has transformed the party into a very powerful political force in opposition to the IRI's rulers. Therefore, the political leadership of the IRI has decided not to fight politically against this party, but to eliminate it physically... Dr. Abdol-Rahman Ghassemlou, who had been Secretary-General of the PDKI since1973, and two of his colleagues, were murdered in Vienna, Austria, at a meeting that had been ostensibly arranged by Iranian officials to discuss a peace settlement. The link between Vienna and Berlin's crime is quite clear.... Undeniable evidence presented at this trial shows clearly the IRI political leadership's decision making and its consequences regarding the elimination of opposition members abroad. The decision to physically eliminate opposition members abroad is the responsibility of an organization called "Special Affairs Committee," which operates under the Supreme Leader's order. Berlin's Mykonos terrorist operation does not have a religious motive. Its motive is only political, and for the sole purpose of staying in power. Presenting a religious cover for this crime and the claim that the IRI is a Representative of God does not change the fact that this crime has been committed on the political grounds of eliminating the opposition. The only aim of this regime

---

23. Mary Williams Walsh, German Court Finds Iran's Leaders Ordered Slayings, THE L.A.TIMES, April 11, 1997, at A1

On April 10, 1997, one-thousand six-hundred and six-ty-five days had elapsed since the night of the Mykonos restaurant assassinations and justice was delivered. This dictum flew higher than the exiles' wildest dreams and expectations, and it reverberated like an explosion: The regime of IRI was proclaimed a "criminal system."

Never before in German legal history had a higher court assigned responsibility to another state in a murder trial while the leaders were still in power.

Germany withdrew its ambassador from Tehran and encouraged other European nations to do the same. By solidarity, all European countries, as well as New Zealand and Australia, suspended diplomatic relations with Iran.

Darabi upon arrival in Iran: Welcoming a terrorist

24. Mykonos Judgment, supra note 27, at 362-63

Survivors' Descriptions of the Terror Attack

Mehdi Ebrahimzadeh's Description

Mehdi Ebrahimzadeh Esfahani was a member of the central council and executive board of the Organization of Iranian People's Majority (Sazman-é Fadaiyan-é Khalq-é Iran-Aksariyat). On the evening of the attack at the Mykonos restaurant, his invitation was not based on his membership in this organization, it was because of his activities as a political activist residing in Berlin. He has written what he recalled from that evening for this book:

On Thursday September 17, 1992, at 8:00pm, I received a phone call from Nouri Dehkordi, who said, "The meeting with the Kurdish leaders is today. There has been a mix up. The Kurds are here at the restaurant and nobody else is here. I do not know why Aziz Ghaffari invited everyone for Friday. It's a disaster, please come over now, as soon as possible."

After a few minutes, the phone rang again. This time, it was Masoud Mirrashed. He had also been invited for Friday, but he was at the Mykonos restaurant for dinner that night simply because he dined there regularly. He was asked to call me by Nouri Dehkordi, requesting I come over as soon as possible, adding that only Parviz Dastmalchi had arrived.

When I arrived at Praguer Avenue, the restaurant had
the only illuminated window on the otherwise dark street.
At the entrance I saw Peter, a regular customer of the restau-
rant, sitting at a table. I said hi to him and then walked to-
ward the back of the restaurant, where another customer
was sitting. Aziz Ghaffari came to greet me and guided me
to the private dining room in the back of the restaurant.
Around a rectangular table were sitting Nouri Dehkordi and
Dr. Sharafkandi. Across from them sat Masoud Mirrashed,
Parviz Dastmalchi, Fattah Abdoli and Homayoun Ardalan.
Nouri introduced me to Dr. Sharafkandi. Sharafkandi asked
Nouri to move and let me sit in his spot. Minutes later, Aziz
Ghaffari, the owner of the restaurant, brought some food to
the table and asked Nouri whether Esfandiar Sadeghzadeh,
who was helping Ghaffari that night, was allowed to sit at
the table and participate to the conversation. Sharafkandi
agreed. So Esfandiar Sadeghzadeh sat at the table as well.
A few minutes later, Aziz Ghaffari joined us, sitting at the
end of the table exactly across from the room's door.

Before the incident, at about 10:50pm, Dr. Sharafkandi,
Parviz Dastmalchi, and Masoud Mirrashed were engaged
in a conversation about Iran's national interests, territorial
integrity, and Kurdish autonomy. Dr. Sharafkandi was ex-
plaining the PDKI's position in favor of autonomy for the
Kurds within Iran. He emphasized that he felt he was just as
Iranian as anyone else. It was at that moment that I saw an
unusual expression on Masoud Mirrashed's face who was
sitting across the table from me. Then I heard somebody
say, in Persian, "You sons of whores!" At the same time
Masoud asked, "Nouri! What's wrong with the doctor?"
Masoud saw something unusual on Dr. Sharafkandi's face.
I look toward the voice coming from Masoud's back. I saw
a man, quite tall, wearing a hood who opened fire immedi-

ately. I realized in a second that this might be a terror attack, targeting us. Instinctively, I pushed Sadeghzadeh with my left hand and pulled Nouri who was on my right-hand side toward myself and under the table. Nouri was leaning on me. Esfandiar went under the table and I, still in my chair, ducked my head underneath. Nouri, who was slumped against me, had been shot as I was pulling him down and his blood was on my shirt, his blood was flowing down on my back. I heard two salvos, a rain of cartridge shells fell to the ground, bottles were clinking, and then there were at least two distinct gunshots. After a long silence, I recovered from the shock and began calling out to the others. I heard Masoud and Parviz answer and opened my eyes. Nouri was still alive. Blood was coming out of his mouth, and he was breathing noisily. Dr. Sharafkandi was lying over Nouri, and Ardalan and Abdoli were in pools of blood on the other side of the table. Ghaffari was on the floor. He was alive.

Parviz and Masoud were trying to get up. Parviz, Masoud, and I found our way out to the front of the restaurant trying not to touch the blood, the shells, or the broken glasses. We wanted to call the police and the ambulance but Peter said he had already called for help. Masoud said he thought that they had closed the restaurant's door, but the door was opened toward the inside of the restaurant. We went out and a few people were pointing in the direction of Praguer Platz.

I called Majid Ebrahimpour, one of the members of The Organization of Iranian People's Majority and asked him to spread the news to the Democratic Party of Iranian Kurdistan's' members. A few minutes later, an ambulance arrived, but it only transferred Nouri to the hospital. We realized that Dr. Sharafkandi, Fattah Abdoli, and Homayoun Ardalan had been killed. A few hours later, when we were at the police station, we found out that Nouri Dehkordi had also passed away, while on the way to the hospital.

Parviz Dastmalchi, April 10, 1997

Parviz Dastmalchi's Description

Parviz Dastmalchi was a member of the supreme council and executive committee of the Republicans of Iran (Jumhurikhahan-é Melliy-é Iran) at the time of the Mykonos murders, but he was invited and present at Mykonos Restaurant for personal reasons, as a political activist residing in Berlin. His account of the evening follows:

I came home after work, around 5:00pm on the afternoon of Wednesday September 16, 1992, and received a voice message on my answering machine from Aziz Ghaffari. He was inviting me to a meeting with the board of the PDKI on Friday at 7:30pm.

The same night, I went to his restaurant for dinner and Aziz asked me whether I got his message and confirmed the date and said that the invitation came on behalf of Nouri Dehkordi.

On Thursday, September 17, 1992, at around 7:50pm, I was planning to read Dr. Sharafkandi's interviews after watching the news on TV, in order to get ready for the meeting the next day. At 8:00pm the phone rang, it was Nouri Dehkordi. He mentioned a misunderstanding about the time of the meeting. He explained that Aziz was supposed to have invited people for Thursday evening, but he had made a mistake and invited them for Friday. He asked me to join them as soon as possible. In the meantime, he was going to contact the other intended guests. I told him I had planned to be there the next day, and I was too tired to join them that night, but he insisted and I agreed to go.

When I arrived at the restaurant, Aziz and the PDKI delegates were arguing about the mistake. The delegates insisted that they could not have told Aziz that the meeting would take place Friday evening since they were, in fact, flying out on Friday morning.

I sat next to Fattah Abdoli, on his right-hand side, and across the table from Dehkordi and Sharafkandi. Aziz Ghaffari was walking around and attending to the guests.

Aside from us, the only other customers present at the Mykonos that night were Peter Böhm, who sat at a table by the entrance, and a young couple who left shortly after Ebrahimzadeh arrived. Also present was a waitress, Maria Voltschanskaya.

After a little while, Masoud Mirrashed arrived and sat on my right-hand side. He had also been invited for Friday, and just happened to come to the restaurant for dinner that night. So Dehkordi invited him to join the party. After him, Mehdi Ebrahimzadeh arrived. He was also invited for Friday night, and came out that night only after Dehkordi had called him. He wanted to sit across the table from us, on the right-hand side of Sharafkandi but at Sharafkandi's request, he sat at Nouri's left-hand side. After him, came Esfandiar Sadeghzadeh. He was not invited to the meeting at all, but joined the group after Aziz Ghaffari asked permission from Dr. Sharafkandi. He sat across the table from Masoud Mirrashed and me, next to Mehdi Ebrahimzadeh, on his left-hand side.

The main topics discussed at the meeting were the situation surrounding the opposition outside of Iran, the PDKI's activities, and how to coordinate those activities. Before the discussion started, we chatted about Iranian assassinations abroad. Sharafkandi said, "If they wanted to kill us, they would, because we are facing a regime that will do anything to remain in power." He added, "Once, I was talking with a peshmerga about life and death in the Kurdistan Mountains. He was sitting on the ground. He stood up and jumped over a bush and said, Kak Saeed, the distance between life and death is just like that."

The dinner was served at around 10:30pm. It was around 10:50pm, while we were eating and talking about Kurdistan. I was looking to the left and in front of me, talking to Sharafkandi when, on my right-hand side, Masoud Mirrashed cut me off and started talking. When I turned slightly to face him, I saw someone stood between him and me. As I was seated, I was not able to see his face and only saw his legs. I thought it might be another guest who had just arrived. What I am describing here only lasted a fraction of a second. As I lifted my eyes, a machine gun appeared just to the right of my face aimed at Dr. Sharafkandi. It started shooting and I even saw the first three cartridge-shells jumping out of the machine gun. I had a glance at the assailant's face. His face was covered with what looked like a handkerchief at the time, but which later turned out to be his sweater. I instinctively threw myself back on the ground and fell on my face and abdomen under the table behind me. In seconds, Fattah Abdoli, the European representative of the Democratic Party of Iranian Kurdistan, who had been sitting on my left-hand side, fell to the ground, about 50-60 cm away from me, face to face. His mouth was full of blood and he was dying. I did not move at all.

In the moment the Islamist Terrorist Abdolrahman Banihashemi, employee of the IRI Ministry of Intelligence, entered the room where we were sitting and stood between Mirrashed and me, Mirrashed could not possibly have seen him. But Dr. Sharafkandi must have seen him and felt the danger, because between the moment I was trying to look at the man and the moment I instinctively threw myself backward, two voices were in my ears. One was Mirrashed, who asked Nouri, "Nouri! What's wrong with Doctor?" The other was the voice of Mehdi Ebrahimzadeh shouting, "Guys! This is a terror attack!"

Two rounds of machine-gun fire were shot and then silence. After the second salvo, without moving, I looked up at where the terrorist was standing to see if the murderer had left, but all of a sudden, I saw an arm with a pistol pointing towards Dr. Sharafkandi. At this time, I realized that there were two people involved, since this person's coat was black and white, while the first person had been wearing a green coat. The idea that he was going to shoot us all crossed my mind. I thought, he is going to shoot Abdoli in the head, and then it will be my turn. But after he shot Sharafkandi in the head, the second shooter went toward Ardalan. Ardalan, who was shot already by the machine-gun, was unconscious but not dead. He came to consciousness for a second and moved his head. And the shooter shot him in the head with a fatal shot. I thought he would shoot Abdoli next and then me, but after a few seconds of silence I heard my name called by Ebrahimzadeh and I came out and asked for help.

I got up and ran to call the police and Peter, the only other customer at the restaurant, said he had already called them. I then called Mehran Barati, one of the intended guests who was invited to the meeting, also mistakenly for the next day, and told him, "We were attacked at the restaurant. I do not know who is dead and who is alive yet, but inform everyone." Then I went back to the private dining room. Fattah Abdoli and Homayoun Ardalan were on the floor and lying in their blood. Sadegh Sharafkandi was also killed but still sitting in his chair. Nouri Dehkordi was leaning on the table, his face against a bier glass. His face and chest were covered in blood and the glass was full of blood. He was still breathing. I went toward him to help. I wanted to hold his face but suddenly I changed my mind. I did not know what to do. I was afraid that any move would cause his death. Aziz Ghaffari, the owner of the restaurant was shot twice, in his leg and abdomen. He automatically stood up and tried to walk, but we stopped him and laid him on the floor.

After a few minutes, firemen and an ambulance arrived at the crime scene. They rushed Nouri and Aziz to the hospital. They examined the corpses and started questioning us right away. After almost two hours, they took us to the Berlin Police Station for deposition. After two hours, my interrogator stepped out of the room and when he came back, he announced that Nouri Dehkordi, the owner of the restaurant has also passed away. I told him that Dehkordi was not the owner of the restaurant. He reflected a bit, called someone, and confirmed that Nouri Dehkordi was dead but Aziz Ghaffari, the owner of the restaurant was alive. The lump in my throat tightened. I could not answer the interrogator any more. He brought me a tranquilizer and left me alone for a while.

It was around 6:00 or 7:00am when I left the interrogation room to go to the washroom. I crossed paths with Shohreh Badiie, Nouri's wife. She hugged me tight and while crying said, "What am I going to do if Nouri dies?" I couldn't tell her that he was dead. I consoled her and said, "I am sure he is ok. Don't worry!"

I went to the washroom, where I saw a mutual friend, Emmanuel Youssefi. I asked him to announce Nouri's death to Shohreh, because I wasn't able to tell her.

At 8:00am, my interrogation was over. I think it was Emmanuel who brought me home in his taxi. I took a hot shower and stood there, flabbergasted, under the hot water for a while. I couldn't do anything.

After a while I called my ex-wife, Parvaneh Teymouri, and explained the whole thing in a few words. I requested that she keep our daughter, Saloomeh, then 12 years old, away from the news. Then I called my brother in Flensburg and asked him to prevent our mother from watching the news. Then I called in sick to my work place at the Red Cross.

I called my friend Werner Kohlhof. He is a board member of Berliner Zeitung, a newspaper leaning toward the Social-Democrat Party of Germany. I briefed him about the attack. He thanked me and said he was in a meeting. I got very confused with his reaction. He said nothing but that indeed he had heard the news and would be in touch. He called me back a second later. He asked me to confirm that I was at the restaurant last night. He apologized for not having understood at first that I was a survivor of the attack.

He asked me to meet him at 10:00 at Café Kranzler in Ku Damn for an exclusive interview.

Werner was waiting for me at Café Kranzler. Although it was a cloudy day, I was wearing dark sunglasses. Not because I did not want to be recognized, but because of the skin injuries from the attack and because my eyes were bruised. In the interview I said that in my opinion, only one group could be behind this terror, the IRI Intelligence and Security Agencies.

My interview was published in the September 19 and 20, 1992 issues of the newspaper. After the interview, I went to the Mykonos restaurant crime scene. Near the restaurant we separated so no one would see us together. There were almost 200 representatives from different local and international media gathered, and no members of the opposition were there to say anything. I reflected for a while and then addressed the ZDF2 reporter and told him that I was one of the survivors of last night's attack. He was extremely interested in interviewing me. He offered me an exclusive interview right away, that he would broadcast to the entire world. The only catch was that I only interview with them. I reflected a bit and declined his offer because the entire international media were there. I apologized and went in front of the restaurant and with a loud voice, asked people to listen. Everybody calmed down and encircled me. As soon as I told them that I was one of the survivors of the attack last night, tens of cameras turned toward me. I spoke shortly. It took only a minute but felt like an eternity. Again, I said that in my opinion, the Islamic Republic of Iran was involved in this terror.

While I was talking to the media, a few Middle Eastern-looking supposed journalists were walking around me. I couldn't hide my fear. I was expecting a knife in my body or throat at any moment. Those days were the days when the "Anonymous soldiers of Imam Zaman" (Murderers sent by the IRI) would kill an Iranian dissident almost every month and nobody ever even protested.

This event started a new page in my fight against the Islamic Republic. By dedicating my life to it, this struggle has definitely changed my life.

The Mykonos Restaurant, Berlin

The Victims

Dr. Mohammad Sadegh Sharafkandi

Dr. Mohammad Sharafkandi was born in Bokan, Iran, on January 11, 1938. He received his degree in chemistry at the Institute of Higher Education in Tehran and went on to study at the University of Sorbonne, Paris, where he received his PhD in analytical chemistry in 1976. While studying in Paris in 1973, he joined the PDKI. After returning to Iran in 1976, while teaching at the Teachers' Higher Training College in Tehran, he became the representative of the PDKI's Secretary-General, Dr. Abdol-Rahman Ghassemlou. In 1980, he became a member of the PDKI Central Committee and was put in charge of the party's operations in Tehran. In the summer of 1980 he moved to the Kurdistan Province in Iran and the Central Committee elected him to be a member of the PDKI's Political Bureau, the highest echelon of the PDKI leadership. He was in charge of the party's publicity efforts. In 1986, he became the PDKI's Deputy Secretary-General and assumed the title of interim Secretary-General after Dr. Ghassemlou's assassination on July 13, 1989. In December, 1991, he was unanimously elected Secretary-General of the PDKI.[25]

25. Zindiginame-i Shuhada [Biography of Martyrs], Bulitan Kurdistan [Kurdistan Bulletin], Nov. 1992, at 18, 18

Homayoun Ardalan

Homayoun Ardalan was born in Saghez, Iran, on February 2, 1950. During the 1979 Revolution, he left his studies at the University of Sanandaj to join the PDKI. He was elected as a member of the Central Committee in 1984 and then became the head of the PDKI Committee in Saghez. After the Eighth Congress, in 1988, he moved to Germany as the PDKI's local representative.[26]

Fatah Abdoli

Fatah Abdoli was born in Naghade, Iran, on April 15, 1961. He joined the PDKI as a student and by 1980, he was one of its most active members. After the Sixth Congress, he served as an alternate member of the Central Committee and as head of the PDKI Committee in Sanandaj, the capital of Kurdistan Province in Iran. At the Seventh Congress, he was elected as a member of the Central Committee and was assigned to head the Committee of Sardasht in Western Azarbayejan, Iran. He succeeded Abdollah Ghaderi as the PDKI's principal representative in Europe, after Ghaderi was assassinated, along with Dr. Ghassemlou and Fazel Rasoul, on July 13, 1989, in Vienna, Austria.[27]

---

26. Zindiginame-i Shuhada [Biography of Martyrs], Bulitan Kurdistan [Kurdistan Bulletin], Nov. 1992, at 18, 20. See also Summary of Facts, supra note 42, at 4

27. Zindiginame-i Shuhada [Biography of Martyrs], Bulitan Kurdistan [Kurdistan Bulletin], Nov. 1992, at 18, 19. See also Summary of Facts, supra note 42, at 4

Nouri Dehkordi, at 23
Picture courtesy of his family

Nourrollah Dehkordi

Nouri Dehkordi was born on March 30, 1946, in Shahr-e Kord, Iran. He left Iran in the 1960s, first travelling to Austria and then, in 1970, to Berlin. While studying in Austria and Germany, he joined the World Iranian Students Confederation, who actively opposed the Shah, advocated freedom for political prisoners, and promoted human rights and democracy. He returned to Iran to participate in the revolution against the Shah in 1979. At the beginning of the revolution, he was co-founder of a new political organization, which advocated socialist ideas, simply named, "Left." After the Islamic Revolution, "Left" became known first as the "Left Union" and later as the "Council of the United Left." In the summer of 1981, he came under investigation for his political activities and was forced to leave his family and go into hiding. In 1982, he went to the Kurdistan Province of Iran to help the PDKI, and then he returned to Germany in 1984, where he was granted political asylum. He was employed by the Red Cross in 1986, as a social worker, and remained politically active. He was a close friend of both Dr. Sharafkandi and his predecessor Dr. Ghassemlou. Although not a professional interpreter or a PDKI activist, he was serving as a translator for the PDKI delegation to the Socialist International Congress as a personal favor to Dr. Sharafkandi.[28]

---

28. Zindiginame-i Shuhada [Biography of Martyrs], Bulitan Kurdistan [Kurdistan Bulletin], Nov. 1992, at 18, 21. See also Summary of Facts, supra note 42, at 4.

Chapter II

The Defendants' Biographies;
More Details of the Terror Attack Plan

Kazem Darabi

Kazem Darabi, who acted as the local henchman for the Mykonos operation, has been identified as an active agent of the IRI Ministry of Intelligence and a member of the Islamic Revolutionary Guard Corps (IRGC).[29]

The defendant Kazem Darabi, was born on March 22, 1959, in Kazeroun, Iran, and is an Iranian citizen. He had resided in Germany since June 6, 1980. His father was a businessman and his mother a home maker. His education goes as far as the end of high school. Although he is a fervent supporter of a fundamentalist Islamic Revolution, after the revolution of 1979 in Iran, he moved to Germany to pursue higher education. He started learning German in Berlin. After a six-month German language class from September 1980 to March 1981, he started attending the

---

29. Grünewald Memo, supra note 32, at 1

university in Hagen and lived close to that city.

He got married in 1985, to a future associate's sister. He has three children; two daughters and one son. His eldest daughter is handicapped.

The German Federal Office for the Protection of the Constitution believes that Darabi served as the conduit between the Islamic Republic of Iran and Hezbollah operatives in Berlin. Indeed, Darabi was heavily involved with the Islamic Student Association of West Berlin (VIS or Anjoman-é Islami-é Daneshjooyan-é Berlin). He became a member of its Executive Board in 1984. At the same time, he also held a leadership position in the "Union of Islamic Student Associations of Europe" (UISAE or Etehadiye-é Islami-é Daneshjooyan-é Oroupa), an organization with a history of violent activism against the opponents of the Islamic Republic. Darabi still retained that position at the time of the Mykonos terror attack.

As an active leader, Darabi has also been a prominent figure at Berlin's Imam Jafar Sadeqh mosque. The German Federal Office for the Protection of the Constitution (BfV) believed this mosque to be strongly associated with Hezbollah sympathizers.[30]

In October, 1988, Darabi purchased a grocery store for the sum of DM85,000.00, in Weserstrasse in Berlin. The Mykonos trial could not trace the source of that money. As he did not have authorization to own a business in Germany, he employed the witness Ayademir to manage the store.

Although the store was destroyed by fire in 1989, the witness Ednan Ayad purchased the store from Darabi in 1990. Darabi still worked there until the end of 1990, and then he became an unofficial shareholder of the Ednan

---

30. Mykonos Judgment, supra note 27, at 189

Ayad Dry Cleaning Company in January, 1991. In 1992, he became an official shareholder, receiving a monthly salary of DM7000.00. He finally obtained an official residency permit on January 19, 1991, and a business permit on May 29, 1991. He started a business named "Darabi and Ayad," which operated between Iran and Germany as an Import-Export company.

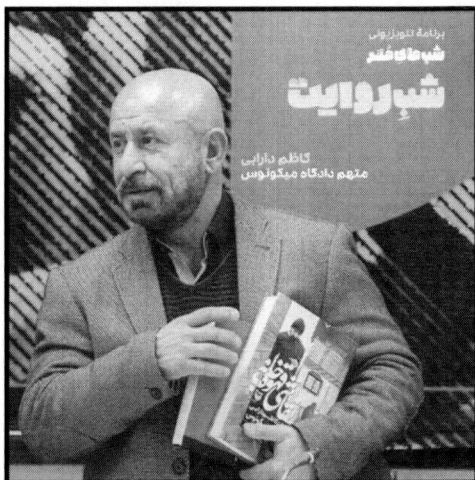

Kazem Darabi, currently living in Iran
*Photo by the Radio and Television of the Islamic Republic of Iran,
November 9, 2009*

Darabi was arrested on October 8, 1992, and according to the investigating judge's warrant on October 9, 1992 he was detained. He was indicted on four counts of murder and one count of attempted murder on May 17, 1993, by Bruno Jost, the German Federal Prosecutor.

Darabi first attracted German security officials' attention in April, 1982, when authorities in Dortmund issued a warrant for his arrest because of his alleged role in an attack on Iranian students opposed to Khomeini, living in the University of Mainz' international student dormitory. These students were violently assaulted by a mob of eighty-six Khomeini sympathizers. This arrest warrant led to his conviction in May, 1982, and his expulsion was ordered by the presiding judge. On June 1st, 1982, the police subpoenaed Darabi to be deported from Germany, based on his having been expelled from the university. Some other Iranian students were expelled at the same time. The expulsion order was appealed by Darabi with help from the IRI Embassy in Bonn, who intervened on his behalf, preventing his expulsion. But according to the verdict, Darabi spent time in a special prison for those residents who were going to be deported from Germany. The Iranian Embassy in Bonn intervened by pressuring the Ministry of Foreign Affairs and the Prime Minister's office in Rheinland-Pfalz, and succeeded in cancelling some of those Iranians' expulsion orders, including Darabi's. Germany agreed to allow some of those Iranians to stay in Germany until they finished their degrees. Important to note here, is that the IRI Embassy was capable of intervening to prevent Darabi's expulsion, even though according to German law, he should have been deported. Darabi was, at that time, single and had not yet enrolled at any school.

After being released, Darabi moved back to Berlin and enrolled at the Technical Professional School of Berlin (Technische Fachhochschule Berlin) in 1983. Darabi was, nonetheless, very unsuccessful as a student. He was expelled, due to poor attendance and for failing his midterm exams. But he succeeded in appealing the decision, and was able to re-enroll for the summer term in 1988.

The IRI Embassy in Bonn had a specific agenda for Darabi. The Embassy tried multiple times to apply for permanent residency permits, for Darabi, and for some other

Iranian students whose permits were conditional and temporary.31 The court concluded that the Embassy had intervened on his behalf so that he could later serve the Islamic Republic's goals.

Darabi is a believer and follower of the Islamic Revolution. He was a member of the IRGC after all. According to the statements of the witness Professor Udo Steinbach, the IRGC is a special unit founded on the values of the Islamic Revolution of Iran. Its responsibilities, "first and foremost," are to defend the Islamic Revolution against opposition at home, export the Islamic Revolution abroad, support the Muslims struggles all over the world, and to fight against the anti-revolutionaries. The IRGC's fights are not just ideological, they are also very violent. Witness Hosseini, member of the board of the Democratic Party of Iranian Kurdistan said that the first time the IRGC attacked Kurdistan, in August, 1979, they killed thousands of people.

Mr. Grunewald, an agent of the Federal Office for the Protection of the Constitution, testified that Darabi was an agent of the IRGC. Mr. Grunewald's information came from reliable sources, and the court accepted the validity of his testimony because in other circumstances his information had been proven correct as well.

Witness C, who had personal experience working in the field, as a former Iranian Intelligence officer when Ayatollah Khomeini had directed assassination operations, provided the court with valuable information regarding Iran's Internal Affairs because of his contacts and relationships with the Intelligence Agencies. He said that in the very early days of the Islamic Republic, in 1979, the IRI sent some IRGC members to Germany, to support a small num-

---

31. Letters from the Embassy on December 11, 1986 and June 26, 1987

ber of Khomeini's supporters. The fact that Darabi arrived in Germany during this period, Mesbahi mentioned in his testimony, ties Darabi to the Islamic Republic's agenda at that time.

As we can understand from the Berlin Education Ministry's letter dated August 14, 1980, Darabi holds a document that is equivalent to a grade 10 high school certificate in Germany. For that reason, he registered as a student in a technical high school in Hagen, in September, 1981, in order to obtain the diploma necessary to attend the technical college afterward. Darabi's application for the college and his registration certificates for the winter and summer terms of 1981-82 illustrates this. Darabi's level of fluency in German is very low. He was registered to a German language learning program at Harnack Schule since entering Germany on April 2, 1980. Due to these facts, and confirmed by his activities, the court concluded that spying had been Darabi's main priority all along.

A-The Grüne Woche (The Green Week)

In January, 1991, Darabi presented himself to the Exhibition's organization as the representative for the IRI's booth at the annual exhibition of crops and livestock in Berlin.

According to the witness Mrs. Watz, manager of the Exhibition, Darabi had been very eager to participate in the show. He managed to present documents very quickly, granting him power of attorney on behalf of the IRI's Consulate in Berlin. Ednan Ayed confirmed this as well.

Mrs. Watz believes that Darabi's power of attorney was granted in an unusual way. It gave him total authorization to act and to use the IRI's name and flag. A representative with such power typically helps assure the Exhibition's organization that the company presented is reliable and that no further consideration is necessary. But none of the above fitted Darabi. He did not even have a personal business permit. Mrs. Watz testified that giving power of attorney to such person, on behalf of the IRI Consulate, was very odd and incomprehensible. We cannot even talk about a reliable company, because Darabi did not have a business at that time. The small grocery store business associated with the witness Ayedmir, president of the Mosque Imam Jaffar Sadegh, burned down and was sold in the last months of 1990. So, during the Green Week exhibition, Darabi did not have any business, reliable or not.

B-Real Estate Transactions for the Consulate General of the Islamic Republic of Iran in Berlin

The Consulate General of the IRI was located in West Berlin, but according to the testimony of Anusek, the previous chief of the Berlin Intelligence Agency (LFV), also a witness in the trial, that Consulate had been shut down because of spying activities. It was later relocated in East Berlin.

In early 1990, the Consul-General assigned Darabi to find a nice house for the relocation of the General Consulate. Darabi then contacted the Erbas real estate company, in order to execute that task. He presented himself as the contact for the General Consulate and behaved as if he was in charge, according to the witness Mr. Erbas. One of the houses presented to Darabi by Mr. Erbas was in Dahlem, Berlin, 67 Podbielskiallee, which is now the location of the General Consulate. Darabi had also been assigned by the General Consulate to find a piece of land for the construction of a Mosque in Berlin.

In a phone conversation between Darabi and the Consul-General Amani Farani, recorded by BfV intercept because of other concerns and according to the Article 10 of the Constitution, the Consul asked "Kazem" Darabi whether or not he had found a location for the construction of the mosque. Darabi responded that he was "looking for a thousand-square-meter piece of land, and he had assigned a few real estate agencies to the task."

The court did not have any doubt regarding the identity of the two persons, because Klaus Grunewald, a BfV agent, testified that a very experienced expert in voice recognition had confirmed their identity based on many other conversations, between the same two, over the phone.

Two days later, on April 26, 1991, Darabi spoke with Mr. Erbas over the phone and this conversation was recorded as well. Darabi inquired about a piece of land for the construction of a mosque and said that the money would be provided through the sale of the Frankfurt Mosque.

Erbas, who in his first interrogation had denied having had any conversations with Darabi regarding the mosque, finally confirmed the content of the conversation with Darabi. Therefore, the validity of the content of the phone conversation between the two men, confirmed by the appraiser of the German Intelligence Agency, was approved by the court.

C-Organizing Rallies

According to Berlin's Intelligence Agency, Darabi organized, with help from Hezbollah, a big rally at Stromstrasse, in Berlin on June 8, 1990, to commemorate the anniversary of Khomeini's death. This fits the testimony of Ayad at trial, who said, *"Everybody in Berlin knows that Darabi is the head of Hezbollah."*

In four photographs taken at this event, Darabi, Amin, Rhayel, and also the witnesses Abdollah, Hassan, and Haidar Hamedani are recognizable. These pictures were found in a handbag that belonged to Rhayel, in Rhine, and were registered as evidence.

The witness Wahabi, the head and agent of the Imam Jaffar Sadegh Mosque, testified that he was assigned, by Darabi, to provide food and drink for six hundred people for the Ashura[32]celebration in 1991, taking place at a rented venue at Stromstrasse. Darabi had covered those expenses.

Wahabi, when asked where Darabi found the money for organizing such event, responded that he did not know. This fact fits the time and the content of a phone call Darabi made to the Consul Amani Farni, on September 9, 1991, recorded by Berlin Intelligence Agency. Over the phone, Darabi said that the issue of finding a venue *"has been taken care of."* The fact that he spoke with Mirkhani, who was also in the Consulate at that time, proves that Darabi had been in contact with the General Consul himself as well.

D-Issuing Passports

A witness in the trial, Haidar Hamedani, testified that he had obtained an Iranian passport with Darabi's help. According to Hamedani's testimony, he only had a German passport to show, a "Fremdenpass," and he wanted to have an Iranian passport as well. Hamedani does not speak Farsi and has no link to Iran other than his Iranian grandfather. The General Consulate in Berlin rejected his inquiry, because they

---

32. The tenth day of Muharram, the first month in the Islamic calendar. It marks the day that Husayn ibn Ali, the grandson of the Islamic prophet Muhammad, was martyred in the Battle of Karbala

thought he was opposed to the Islamic Republic. When Darabi found out about it, he promised Haidar he would find
a way to obtain a passport for him, because Haidar was a
supporter of the Islamic Republic. Darabi paid DM350.00
for Haidar and his brother Hassan Hamedani, intervening
on their behalf to obtain their passports. Hassan Hamedani
needed a new passport because there were some "concerning" stamps on his passport. Nonetheless, Darabi managed
to obtain both passports in three weeks' time.

As expected, when put on the stand Haidar and Hassan
Hamedani refused to confirm what they had stated during
their previous interrogations, and testified differently. They
joined those witnesses who pretended that their memory was
failing them or claimed that there had been a misunderstanding. Under various pretexts, they refused to tell the truth.

E-Darabi's Activities as a Student

Darabi was sitting on the board of the "Islamic Student Associations of West Berlin (VIS)," and also the "Union of
Islamic Student Associations in Europe (UISAE)," which
covered 30 different councils. UISAE and the member
councils became a firmly pro-Khomeini propaganda organization after the Islamic Revolution of 1979, with the
mandate of expanding the Islamic reign to the entire world.

The witnesses Rositalab, Sabet, Ameli, Bahman Berenjian, and Zavareh were also members of the VIS. They
confirmed and testified in court that UISAE's goal was to
advance the ideology of the Islamic Republic of Iran, in-
fluencing universities by organizing rallies with a political
and religious agenda, and through publishing books, magazines, newspapers, and manifestos.

They also testified in court that the UISAE's activities

included gathering news and intelligence, identifying opponents of the IRI, and combating the activities of Iranian opposition figures.

But the UISAE's goals and responsibilities were not just limited to these activities. According to the Federal Intelligence Agency's witness Mr. Grunewald, and the Berlin Intelligence Agency's witness Mr. Anusek, and also Mesbahi's testimony (Witness C), these Islamic student organizations are supposed to not only gather information, but act against the opposition members as well. This is exactly the reason why the UISAE and its member councils are in close contact with radical Islamic groups such as Hezbollah, in addition to official Iranian authorities and institutions, such as embassies and cultural offices.

Mesbahi offered the court with complementary intelligence in this regard. He knew a lot from personal experience about the UISAE activities. Concerning the true nature of the UISAE and the Islamic centres, Mesbahi gave answers which matched the expert testimonies of Professor Udo Steinbach. Since 1979, as a student in Paris, and then both as the Chief of Intelligence at the Iranian Embassy in France and even after his deportation from France in 1984 because of spying activities, Mr. Mesbahi was the agent responsible for managing the different intelligence agencies in Western Europe, until 1985. This kind of position is usually the Consulate's responsibility. But according to Mesbahi, until 1983, all employees of the Embassy were free to decide whether or not to participate in Intelligence activities.

In fact, the UISAE had been managed by the Ministry of Culture and Islamic Guidance since 1984. This Ministry itself is under the umbrella of the Islamic Revolutionary Guard Corps. The UISAE works for the Office of Intelligence of the IRGC, and its board of directors' members are designated by the Supreme Leader of Iran himself.

In 1984, when the Ministry of Culture and Islamic Guidance officially took over the UISAE, the union acted as a reliable source of intelligence and security for the IRI Intelligence Agency's spying activities. Darabi himself was actively involved in gathering information on opposition members and students in tandem with the IRI Embassy.

The witness Saghafi tried to downplay the importance of Darabi's ties to the Embassy, saying that it was very common for all members of the VIS and UISAE to have ties with the Iranian Embassy.

According to Bahman Berenjian and Zavareh, Darabi had an important role in organizing rallies and inviting guest speakers to their events. According to Berenjian's testimony, Darabi became a board member of the VIS on July 5, 1984, and later became the Chief of the UISAE in Europe, the public relation officer, responsible for organizing rallies and meetings. He had been working for the VIS until his arrest on October 8, 1992.

Mesbahi, as the former mediator and manager of all the IRI Intelligence Agencies in Europe, was also responsible for the Islamic organizations. For that reason, he travelled a few times to the General Consulate of Iran in Hamburg. The General Consulate was managed at that time by Mr. Farhadnia, who was a spy for the Intelligence Agency and had close ties with fundamentalist groups such as Hezbollah. Mesbahi testified on the stand that at least three times, while Mesbahi was in a meeting with the General Consul, Darabi entered the room without knocking and whispered something to Farhadnia's ear.

All these facts prove very close ties between Kazem Darabi and the Intelligence Agencies of the Islamic Republic of Iran.

In a phone conversation between Darabi and the IRI Consul-General in Berlin, on April 24, 1991, recorded by BfV telephone intercept, the Consul Mohammad Amani-Farani inquired about a Kurdish-Iranian student, a member of the Kurdish student union and the Iranian opposition, who studied at the Free University of Berlin. Darabi promised to take care of the matter by conducting surveillance on the student.

According to the witness Grunewalde, the student mentioned was indeed a member of the "Union of Kurdish Students," and was an opposition member. Therefore, there is no doubt that Darabi had the mission to isolate and identify opposition members, which is a designated task of the Intelligence Services.

G-Organizing an Antagonist-Rally

In June, 1991, a group of 50 to 60 people gathered in front of the Iranian General Consulate in Berlin East at Stavangerstraße, to protest against the Islamic Republic and to demand the immediate release of political prisoners. Darabi led a group of 15 individuals, Iranian and Lebanese, in protest against this rally. Darabi's group chanted, "Death to America" and "Allah-o-Akbar" (God is great).

Regarding this event, the court accepted the testimony of the witness Nowzarinehzad. There was no doubt that he was himself an opposition member, he followed the trial on behalf of the "Iranian Refugees Council- Berlin." This witness delivered a very clear narrative, describing this rally and anti-rally without any bias. His statements highlighted the fact that Darabi and the others did not use violence in their

104 anti-protest, which reinforced the witness's impartiality.

H-Cultural Festival 1991

Amin, the terrorist who guarded the door during the Mykonos Restaurant attack, said, when interrogated, that Darabi
had spoken of an Iranian Cultural Festival in Dusseldorf
and that there might be some issues with 'Monafeghins'.
The word 'Monafeghins' has always been used by the IRI
Officials to describe the opposition group MEK.[33] Amin
also said that Lebanese citizens living in Berlin were in
possession of guns, gas pistoles, and gas sprays.

The court examined these testimonies and concluded the following: From September 12, 1991 until October
13, 1991, in Dusseldorf, an Iranian Cultural Festival was
organized. The organizer was the Ministry of Culture and
Islamic Guidance of the Islamic Republic of Iran, and the
Minister himself was present. The MEK supporters had
a book booth across the street from the festival location.
They were displaying pictures of political prisoners who
had been executed by the IRI. In this way, they were protesting against the actions of the Islamic Republic of Iran.

Darabi was contacted by someone from "Iran House"
(Khaneh-é Iran) in Köln, giving him instructions to gather some 'Arab friends' from Berlin and go to Dusseldorf.

---

33. The People's Mojahedin Organization of Iran, or the Mojahedin-é Khalq
sâzmân-é mojâhedîn-é khalq-é îrân, abbreviated MEK, PMOI, or MKO, is an
Iranian political-militant organization based on Islamic and Marxist ideology.
It advocates overthrowing the Islamic Republic of Iran's leadership and
installing its own government. The MEK was the "first Iranian organization
to systematically develop a modern revolutionary interpretation of Islam – an
interpretation that differed sharply from both the old conservative Islam of
the traditional clergy and the new populist version formulated in the 1970s by
Ayatollah Khomeini and his government.".

Darabi executed the order. He recruited a group of his Lebanese friends, including Amin's and Rhayel's friends, and others such as Adnan Ayad, the witnesses Hassan and Haidar Hamedani, Arabi-Balaghi, Moussa Hassan, Nassredin, Fanayesheh, Schiele, and Hossein Konj. They all travelled by bus from a mosque in Berlin to Dusseldorf. But Darabi drove alone to Osnabruck and picked up Haidar, on the way to Dusseldorf.

According to Amin's testimony in court, they armed themselves with pistols, gas guns, and mace. Darabi had been the liaison between the Iranian and the Lebanese individuals who were helping him. Amin added that during the festival, a fight started between their group and the opposition members and a few people were injured.

Darabi and his accomplices, along with other Iranians who were already present at the Dusseldorf festival, attacked the MEK supporters as soon as they arrived at the location on September 29, 1991. They chanted *"Allah-o-Akbar,"* *"Khomeini Rahbar (leader),"* and *"Death to Monafeghin* (MEK),"* while breaking the book and picture exhibition booth. They assaulted members of the Iranian opposition group MEK with wooden and metallic sticks and released gas sprays. Several MEK members were seriously injured. Eye witnesses later testified to the apparent leadership role Darabi played in the assault.

Only one assailant among the Lebanese, Tarik Shiele, who was the most violent, was injured. Darabi assumed the responsibility of taking care of him. He visited him at the hospital many times and, after a while, transferred Shiele to Osnabruck with Haidar's help.

The request made to Darabi from (Khaneh-é Iran) in Köln, to gather some people to protest against MEK, was recorded by a Federal Intelligence Service (BfV) telephone tap.

I-Board of Directors of the Centre for Islamic Unity

In 1989, Darabi had been the second-in-charge on the board of directors for the Centre for Islamic Unity, located at 125 Reichenberger in Kreuzberg, Berlin. The first-in-charge was the witness Zavareh.

The Centre for Islamic Unity was founded in 1987. According to its by-laws, its mandate is not only realized in religious statutes, but also in establishing contact and collaboration with the Islamic Unions of Berlin. This Centre, just like the Islamic Centre of Hamburg, serves the purposes of propagating Fundamentalist Islamic thoughts, such as the founding a "Totalitarian Kingdom of God" on earth, and gathering intelligence and information.

Darabi and other activists of the Centre for Islamic Unity were dependent on the VIS.

The Centre stopped all activity in 1990, but was replaced by the Mosque Imam Jaffar Sadegh, located in Koloniestraße in Berlin. It is now a place for the fundamentalist Shi'ites who have adopted its mandate.

The facts expressed here were brought to light by the Court of Administrative Affairs at Charlutenburg Palace. They are the result of studying the documents produced by these Centres and Unions, hearing the testimonies of Grunwalde and Anusek about the beginning and end of the activities of the Centre for Islamic Unity, the intelligence work of Professor Udo Steinbach, and the witnesses Bahman Berenjian's and Mesbahi's testimonies.

J-Darabi's Activities at the Mosque

The Mosque Imam Jaffar Sadegh, which moved to Koloniestraße, Berlin, in summer of 1992, had in fact replaced the Centre for Islamic Unity located in Reichenburgstraße. This mosque was not just a place of worship, but also a place to exchange intelligence information, and for the development and promotion of the Islamic Revolution. It was designed to reach out to, and organize activities with, other Muslim groups.

Statements from Anusek, along with intelligence gathered by the Intelligence Services of Berlin, confirm that this mosque served as Hezbollah's main base in Germany.

In July, 1990, a protest was organized at this mosque in collaboration with Hezbollah. The IRI's Ambassador to Germany and the Executive Chief of the Hamburg Islamic Centre also participated in the planning.

Darabi was not only participating in religious activities. He was very active politically as well. Many witnesses confirm this fact. For example, Wahabi testified that Darabi was very respected at the mosque, and that he organized many celebrations, as well as funerals. The witnesses Arabi Bolaghi and Alirezai spoke much more carefully about him, and testified merely that Darabi was very well known in Islamic circles. But the most accurate of them all was the accused Adnan Ayad, who spoke of Darabi during his interrogation session. Ayad, without having any reason to exaggerate, said that Darabi was the Chief of Hezbollah in Berlin and everybody knew it.

Indeed, the fact that Darabi incited people to protest and gave speeches about the Islamic Revolution at different mosques and events confirms the importance of his involvement in political activities.

According to witnesses Dhaini and Brestrich, Darabi participated in protests against Salman Rushdi in Berlin, and in Bonn as well. In fact, Darabi consulted even with Brestrich about the choice of slogans.

The court concluded that Darabi had been a very active supporter of the Islamic Republic of Iran in every angle of his activities. For 12 years, he had dedicated himself to the Islamic Republic with perseverance, sacrifice, and an ability to accomplish different tasks. Darabi's aptitude for executing difficult and complicated assignments, and using violence when necessary, is one of his most significant traits.

Because of his position as a businessman, Darabi was easily able to spy on opposition members, without arousing suspicion. When the General Consulate of the IRI was shut down in West Berlin, Darabi continued to gather intelligence. Under the cover of religious activities, he was able to connect with the Lebanese fundamentalists, and to determine how trustworthy they were in their views about the IRI. These characteristics enabled Darabi to organize the murder of the leaders and representatives of the Democratic party of Iranian Kurdistan, and at the same time limit the exposure of the IRI Ministry of Intelligence's assets, misleading the investigators.

K-Darabi's Motivation for the Execution of the Assignment

Darabi's main motive for accepting the assignment to organize this crime can be deduced from his personality and behaviour. Darabi's demeanor and character left the Court no doubt that he had accepted the assignment from the IRI and organized it.

The Court didn't even consider the testimonies of the Witness B, because some doubt existed regarding their validity.

Darabi was regarded as the Chief by the local individuals participating in the terror attack. The accused individuals Amin, Rhayel, and Haidar, were directly involved in the crime. Ali Sabra bought the getaway car, and the accused Atris forged a passport for Rhayel. The Hit Team, led by Sharif, checked in and coordinated all details with Darabi, from the moment they landed in Berlin until the final details of the plan were decided and confirmed. Such coordination with Darabi was absolutely necessary, because the leader of the team had to know all about the supplies and logistics before deciding the final steps of the terror attack.

The report of the German domestic security agency (BfV) to the Court dating December 19, 1995, included information that the Hit Team had coordinated everything through an unnamed henchman in Berlin. This information came from a very reliable intelligence source who had worked with Germany's Intelligence Agencies before. This source was not the Witness C, Mesbahi.

The witness Klaus Grunwalde became personally convinced of the exactitude of the source of this information after having a very detailed conversation with the source themselves, and by studying the file on February 5, 1996.

The terror attack plan and Darabi's role in it were once again confirmed by Mesbahi's testimony. The witness first stated that he was in possession of valuable information about the command structure and decision making within the Iranian State, with regard to terror attacks. He also had information and research data identifying agents Moghadam, Ershad, Kamali, and important information about Banihashemi (Sharif). But he knew nothing about the exact plan for this act of terror, nor Darabi's specific role. He did not know if the local henchman was directly involved in the crime.

Nonetheless, Mesbahi's information proved crucial, in the sense that he explained the modus operandi of the general execution of these terrors. His explanations gave the court a background on which to examine the Mykonos case. The comparison led to the conclusion that Mykonos terror attack had been conducted in a manner consistent with methods previously used by the Islamic Republic of Iran.

Witness Mesbahi explained that in these kinds of terror plots, each and every one of the people involved, the Iranian General Consulate, the local henchman, and the Hit Team arriving from Iran, had a very particular role.

He also confirmed that, according to his knowledge in 1992, the Iranian Embassy in Bonn was not the only source of intelligence for the Ministry. The Iranian Consulate in Frankfurt had been another Spy Cell for the Iranian regime. The heads of these Spy Cells are in connection with the "Special Affairs Council," but they avoid any direct contact with the Hit Team. These bases are responsible for determining what is feasible, and ensuring logistics for the Hit Team. The Consulates, in order to avoid all contact with the Hit Team, usually use a trusted person from outside the Consulate to provide support logistics for the Hit Team. Therefore, the Hit Team do not reside in a hotel but in a safe house chosen and secured by that trusted henchman.

According to Mesbahi, for operations abroad, they usually use members of Hezbollah. This is in perfect accordance with the testimony heard from the witnesses Chehade and Mohammed Javadeh. These individuals complained that the Islamic Republic of Iran always uses members of Hezbollah for such terrorist operations abroad.

Of course, later on, Chehade tried to change his testimony. He then said that what he meant was that his compatriots do not participate in these operations, but they are unfairly suspected.

Mesbahi added that once the Hit Team is chosen for the operation, the leader of the team is free to decide how he would like it conducted. Mesbahi said that he had heard directly from Banihashemi, saying that after the operation he had fled to Iran by airplane, as is usual for the Hit Team.

The Court was able corroborate Mesbahi's statements. His information about the usual preparation methods for a terror operation was based on his own Intelligence-Security activities role in regard to the failed terror attack on Hadi Khorsandi, the Iranian Poet residing in London, England. His information was also in perfect accordance with Amin's confessions, with respect to the roles of Sharif and Darab.

All the witnesses' testimonies, confessions, and the demeanor of the people involved in the Mykonos terror team combined still did not provide proof that Darabi had received a direct order involving this murder. Even Amin, who had directly participated in the attack, did not know all the facts. For example, Amin did not know anything about the murder weapons, nor the getaway car. Nonetheless, the Court was able to connect all the dots, concluding that Darabi was the henchman, directly responsible for logistics involved in the preparation of this terror attack, based on documents and on Darabi's activities.

L-Darabi's Decision to Flee

According to witnesses Liedrowski and Adnan Ayad, Darabi had decided to fly to Iran between October 8 and 10, 1992. He had even bought his ticket. Adnan said that the departure was for business purposes. Adnan referred to a letter from the Abrishamsaz Company, dated October 8, 1992, asking Darabi to go to Iran, to visit the firm and to confirm his order of clothing and other products. But this letter proved nothing, because it could have been written with the purpose of justifying Darabi's return to Iran.

Plus, the letter was proven to have been made up out of two different parts, put together. One part was the title of the company, and the other part was written with another font. The letter was a copy sent by fax.

The Court referred to the report from the BKA, dated July 27, 1995, according to which the stated Company had never existed. On the other hand, the BKA could prove that all documents issued by the so-called Company were fake. Therefore, the fact that Adnan Ayad lied that Darabi's trip to Iran would have been a simple business trip, and tried to prove that by presenting a counterfeit letter, makes all his other confessions untrustworthy.

The fact is that when Amin and Rhayel got arrested on October 14, 1992, and when the media reported, on October 7, 1992, that the police found Rhayel's palm print on the murder weapon (the Colt), Darabi seriously thought of leaving Germany, but he didn't.

On April 10, 1997, Kazem Darabi Kazerouni was convicted and sentenced to life imprisonment. The judgment concluded that: *"Darabi... organized the killings for the Iranian secret service. He knew the goal and willingly participated in the destruction of four human lives."*

Abbas Rhayel

Abbas Rhayel was born in Lebanon, on November 12, 1967, and grew up in Beirut. He is a Lebanese national.
He spent his childhood in Beirut with his family. His father owned a big grocery store and Rhayel, who had a very close relationship with his father, used to help in the family business. It is not clear how many siblings he had, because sometimes he spoke of 2 and sometimes of 8 other siblings. Rhayel had been in school from 1973 to 1983, but he had

Abbas Rhayel, convicted terrorist in Mykonos assassination
Currently living in Iran

no real job. He was only helping his father in the family business, and later helping his mother, after his father passed away. He also replaced his brother, for a short period of time, in an office.

Rhayel left Lebanon accompanied by Amin, Ali Sabra, and a few other Lebanese fellows. They entered Germany through Munich and Rhayel settled first in Aachen, in 1989, along with his friend Amin. They registered as refugees. He intended to study Auto-Mechanics and work in that field. Then he moved to Berlin, because of uncomfortable conditions in Aachen, but the police forced him to return to Aachen. Rhayel defied a police order and stayed in Berlin. Rhayel twice applied for political asylum, unsuccessfully. On the third occasion he submitted a fraudulent application using false documents, in the name of Imad Ammash, provided by his mother. He was granted a temporary residency permit in this name, which extended until March 18, 1992.

Rhayel first lived with his compatriots, such as the witnesses Mehdi Chahrour and Hossein Chamas, and made a living working part-time at the local restaurant, "Habibi," at a car-wrecker, at a flea market (Flohmarkt), and at Darabi's grocery store. All while receiving social welfare benefits. He also did some car dealing for his brother in Lebanon.

He and Amin filed a refugee request in Switzerland, which was not granted, and he was deported to Lebanon by the police on March 20, 1991. After a short period of time he returned to Berlin and continued to live in the house that belonged to Darabi, at 64B Detmolderstraße in Wilmerzdorf. Darabi only used this house occasionally. Darabi's brother, Ghassem, also lived in this house for a while. Rhayel was very religious and observed Islamic rules literally. He stayed in Darabi's house even after Darabi's brother went back to Iran in 1992. In May, 1992, the German authorities again ordered Rhayel to leave the country. Although he received transit papers from the German authorities, he did not take the opportunity to leave voluntarily. Rhayel was arrested for his alleged involvement in Mykonos assassinations on October 4, 1992, in the home of Youssef Amin's brother, in Rheine, while he and Amin were preparing for their escape.

Rhayel was detained on October 5, 1992, in accordance with an arrest warrant issued by the Investigating Judge of the Federal Ministry of Justice.

Rhayel is the terrorist who shot Ardalan once in the back of his head, and Sharafkandi twice in the head, and once in the neck. Rhayel's final shots were unnecessary to Sharafkandi. Ardalan was shot four times in the chest. The subsequent forensic examination revealed that Ardalan might have survived but for the final shot to his head.

Abbas Hossein Rhayel was convicted and sentenced to

life in prison. The court found Rhayel guilty of firing some of the fatal shots.

Youssef Mohamad El-Sayed Amin

Yousef Amin was born on November 5, 1967, in Adaissi, Lebanon. He is a Lebanese national. He first lived in his birth city, with his family of 14 siblings. Three of his brothers worked in a bank and another one was the chief of a prison. It is not clear what his father did for a living, but his mother was a homemaker.

Amin started training as a carpenter, after finishing his second year of elementary school. Later on, he moved to Beirut with his family, and went to a technical public school from 1977 to 1983. Due to chaotic life conditions because of the civil war, he did not finish school. At that time, he could not even properly read or write. He only learned how to write and read through private lessons at age of 20. Then he went to school for six months to become a plumber and started working in that field.

He got married for a short period of time, in 1989. According to Amin, he got divorced because of pressure from his in-laws, who were fundamentalist Islamists. They accused him of working with the Amal organization.

Because of the civil war, and chaotic life conditions, in Lebanon, Amin decided to leave and go to Germany. He travelled with two others from the Mykonos attack team, Rhayel and Ali Sabra (Sabra is still a fugitive), as well as the trial-witness Ali El Moussavi, and two other young men. They flew to Hungry and, with help of smugglers, after a lot of trouble, finally arrived in Germany at the end of 1989. Once in Germany, they settled in Aachen. After a while, Amin and Rhayel moved to Berlin together. Amin applied for asylum for the first time on February 1, 1990. He later withdrew his application for asylum, on April 9, 1990, and received only a temporary permit to reside in Berlin. His permit was extended, for the last time, until March 5, 1992.

Youssef Amin, convicted terrorist in Mykonos assassination
Member of Hezbollah, Trained in Iran

Amin stayed first in a refugee camp at Tegel, Berlin, and later moved to Darabi's house, staying with Rhayel, at 64B Detmolderstraße in Wilmersdorf, Berlin. He made a living by receiving welfare benefits and working for Darabi. He worked for six months at Darabi's grocery store with Adnan Ayad, at the Adnan-Darabi Laundry, and at the Green Week Exposition. He also spent some time working in the kitchen of the "Habibi" restaurant. The restaurant was a meeting place for his Lebanese compatriots.

Amin and Rhayel decided to move to Switzerland in 1990. They filed an asylum request, because they heard that the welfare benefits for refugees were better in Switzerland. In Switzerland, Amin received, monthly, SF850 from social security and 700 for his rent, but he would go back to Berlin from time to time, to receive benefits and extend his residence permit there as well. Ultimately, the Swiss authorities denied them asylum. Amin and Rhayel were deported to Lebanon from Switzerland on March 20, 1991. Amin got married again. His wife currently lives in Lebanon.

Amin got back to Berlin with help of a smuggler in Prague. His wife arrived in Germany as well, in November, 1991. They lived with Amin's brother, Ahmad Amin, at his place in Rheine, in the west of Germany. Amin mostly stayed in Rheine, but travelled very often to Berlin, to collect his social security allocations and to participate in the religious ceremonies at the Imam Jaffar Sadegh's mosque.

Berlin Police ordered Amin to leave Germany on June 19, 1992. He appealed the court's decision, but his appeal was rejected and he was given the order to leave Germany voluntarily, an order that he ignored. In December, 1992, he became a father.

Amin and Rhayel were arrested on October 4, 1992, at Amin's brother's home in Rheine. He was detained on October 5, 1992, in accordance with the arrest warrant issued by the Investigating Judge of the Federal Ministry of Justice.

Amin was guarding the door of the Mykonos Restaurant at the time of the attack, ensuring the hit team would not be disturbed, as they sought out their targets in the restaurant.

Amin was found guilty in the Mykonos trial as an accessory to the four murders, and for aiding and abetting an attempted murder. He was sentenced to eleven years in prison.

Documents relating Amin and Rhayel to Lebanon Hezbollah and their training in Iran

The witness Ismail El Moussavi was a member of Hezbollah from 1983 to 1988. He testified under oath that he had been with Amin and Rhayel, in 1986, while training in Iran, in Rasht City by the Caspian Sea, at an IRGC Training Camp. He explained that the training included military diving, along with courses in religious ideology and religious history. He also mentioned that only the most dedicated members of Hezbollah were accepted for these programs. Amin and Rhayel were both zealous Shiites and followers of the Fundamentalist Islamist Revolution of Iran.

Hossein Konj testified similarly, saying that he knew Amin and Rhayel from their training for Hezbollah.

El Moussavi testified that Amin had a few accidents during the militia training, and that he could not swim very well. For this reason, Amin was asked to leave the training program and return to Lebanon. But he begged them to stay and continue the training. His request was granted, but nevertheless, he did not finish the training successfully.

The witness Ismail El Moussavi only gave a very brief explanation regarding Hezbollah's organizational structure and leadership, without mentioning any details. He was careful not to give away any information that would endanger the organization.

The Court did not accept El Moussavi's testimony, partly because of what he said, but also because what he said was established in documents as well. Documents released by the Federal Intelligence Service (Bundesnachrichtendienst) proved that Amin and Rhayel received training in military diving in Iran. These documents confirmed El Moussavi's testimony.

The existence of a training camp in Rasht, Iran, for the purpose of training Hezbollah members, was testified to by El Moussavi, Hossein Konj, and also President Banisadr. President Banisadr confirmed that these camps started operating during his presidency. The witness Mesbahi, as a former spy for the IRI Intelligence and Security Agency, also knew about the existence of the militia. He testified that this camp is allocated to naval military training and that it trains Hezbollah members.

El Moussavi's information was also confirmed by the testimonies of Hossein Konj and his brother, Shavoki Konj. The two brothers testified that they had seen Rhayel and Amin, at a Hezbollah Naval Base in Hay-Madi, close to Beirut, while the brothers themselves had been stationed there. According to them, that base only housed militia who were training as divers.

An anecdote told by another witness, Rachid Jaradeh, also confirmed these statements. Apparently, he had been traveling to Bad Hamburg, to go the Moussa Sadr's wedding with Amin, Rhayel, and Majdi Chahrour, when Jaradeh had criticized Hezbollah. Chahrour reminded Jaradeh not to criticize Hezbollah in Rhayel's presence, because Rhayel was a Hezbollah fighter who had been trained at a Naval Base in Iran. The witness Wahabi also testified that Amin had told him about his training in Iran.

After these testimonies, Amin finally confessed that he had been at the Naval Base in Iran.

The witnesses Ibrahim and Ismail El Moussavi, and Hossein Konj, stated that all Hezbollah militia have nicknames. Amin's nickname is "Aboo Mohamad" and Rhayel's nickname is "Rhagheb." Amin had also called himself "Beheshti." Beheshti is the name of a Shiite Leader

(Ayatollah), who was said to have been assassinated by anti-revolutionaries soon after the Iranian revolution. People close to Amin and Rhayel knew them by their nicknames as well.

According to Ibrahim El Moussavi, Ali Sabra, the terrorist who bought the getaway car, was also a member of Hezbollah since 1984. Ali Sabra's nickname was "Aboo Moussa."

Mohammad Atris

Mohammad Atris was the oldest of five siblings, with three sisters and one brother. He was born on February 10, 1970 in Chihine, Lebanon. He grew up in an area west of Beirut, with his family. His father was a businessman, and his mother was a homemaker. Atris went to a French school, "Francine Soeurs," that belonged to the church. He attended this school from 1974 to 1978 and graduated with a Lebanese diploma. He had the intention of studying Industrial Economics, but because of unrest in Lebanon, he could not pursue his dreams.

As there was no prospect for a bright future for him in Lebanon, he decided to leave. The idea became stronger as he felt more pressure to join the army and fight for the Lebanese National Movement. He did not want to join the Movement, although they had control over the area of the country where he lived. He claimed that he left Lebanon when the Movement kidnapped his father and forced him to join the fight. His brother, Chauki Atris, left Lebanon in February, 1989, and joined their uncle in Berlin. Mohammad followed, with the rest of his family, a month later. His father joined them by the end of the same year.

The Atris family first filed an asylum request in Germany, and then later withdrew it. They were allowed to stay in Germany as residents. The Atris family had enough money, and in Berlin they received financial help, so they did not have any financial problems. They rented a house in Wedding, Berlin. The accused, Mohammad Atris, only went to a German language school for a month, but even outside of the school, he learned to speak German very well. He obtained a work permit in 1990, after which he started working in the Steakhouse Berlin. The witness Mahmoud Ali Alian testified that he worked with Atris at the Steakhouse Berlin until 1991, then the Mendoza Steakhouse until 1992, and they worked together for another two months in a pizzeria. After that, Atris stopped working, and received DM500.00 as his welfare benefits allocation. While initially he was interested in sports, clubbing, women, and cars, his interests shifted gradually toward Islam. Like the others involved in the Mykonos attack, he went regularly to the mosque. He prayed and he wanted to get to know the accused Amin, because Amin's family were the descendants of the Muslim's Prophet Mohammad.

Atris was arrested, according to a warrant issued by the investigating judge on October 7, 1992, on suspicion of forging documents used to help the Mykonos perpetrators escape, but he was released without charge. Another arrest warrant was issued on January 27, 1993. Atris was arrested again, charged with assisting with the Mykonos assassination plot, and with preparing forged documents intended to help Rhayel escape the country after the attack.

Mohammad Atris was convicted of being an accessory to the murders. He was sentenced to five years and three months in prison.

Ataollah Ayad

Ataollah Ayad was born in 1966, in Borghammoud, Lebanon. According to him, he is a country-less Palestinian. He became a member of the Palestinian Democratic Front at age ten. In 1979, after having finished grade 5 at elementary school, he started his military training in Syria.

He fought against Israel from Lebanon. After the Palestinian Democratic Front withdrew from Lebanon in 1982, Ayad joined the Amal militia in 1993. He started fighting against Israel and Hezbollah, as a leader and commander of Amal. He was injured 3 times.

Ataollah Ayad

Ayad became a refugee, in Germany, in 1990, and resided in Berlin. There are a few narratives about his escape. According to himself, he was threatened by Hezbollah. But according to witnesses, he has been expelled from Amal because of his wrong doings and his general demeanor.

His wife and his two children arrived in Berlin two

months after he did. Their third child was born in Germany. One of his children suffered from paralysis. Ayad's family only had a temporary residence permit, and they were supposed to leave Germany in 1991, but they didn't.

Ayad was arrested on December 9, 1992. He was detained from December 10, 1992 until August 28, 1995, in accordance with an arrest warrant issued by the Investigating Judge of the Federal Ministry of Justice. Ataollah Ayad was acquitted and released after being remanded in custody, pending trial, for four years.

Farajollah Haidar (aka Abu Jafar, aka Faraj)

Haidar was born on January 1, 1965, in Lebanon. When his family returned on October 22, 1992, his wife told the authorities that Haidar was still in Lebanon. Further investigation showed that he had already left Lebanon for Iran, where his family later joined him.

Haidar drove the getaway car for the assassination team. BfV had previously identified him as a key member of Hezbollah in Osnabruck.

He was not arrested. He abruptly left Germany, with his family, destined for Beirut, on September 25, 1992, presumably to evade arrest.

Mohammad

Mohammad is only known by his first name. He is an Iranian national who has never been fully identified. He presumably acted as a spotter for the Mykonos team. On the night of the murders, Mohammad was keeping watch on the restaurant. He called the team's operational base—at

Senftenberger Ring 7—at about 9:00pm, to inform Bani-hashemi that all of the targets had arrived at the restaurant and that the operation could proceed as planned. Moham-mad reportedly left Germany for Iran immediately after the assassination.

Ali Dakhil Sabra

Ali Sabra had served in Hezbollah alongside Amin and Rhayel. He came with them to Germany, where he applied for asylum.

Ali Sabra procured the BMW getaway car used by the assassination team.

He was not arrested, and on October 20, 1992, he withdrew his asylum application and flew to Lebanon, presumably to evade arrest.

Chapter III

Darabi's Logistic Support

The Local Team

As a volunteer servant to the Islamic Republic of Iran's interests, a member of the IRGC, and a follower of the principles of the Islamic Revolution, Darabi was highly incentivized and interested in the mission assigned to him. He was under no undue threat or obligation to carry out the assassination plan. He believed in the Islamic Republic, and in its policy of eliminating the opposition in order to strengthen itself. Darabi did not need a direct order.

In order to fulfill his mission, Darabi started gathering people he could trust. He knew the accused, Amin, Rhayel, and Ali Sabra, because of their membership in Lebanese Hezbollah. They were quite close as friends. Darabi even found jobs for the accused Rhayel. He hired Rhayel in his own business, and Darabi allowed him to stay at his house at Detmolderstrasse 64B. Amin lived in that house for a while as well. But the reason Rhayel and Amin accepted their roles in the Mykonos terror plot was not based on a perceived debt to Darabi. They, as members of Hezbollah, had the same ideology as the Islamic Republic, and they worked toward achieving the same goals. They also wanted to help strengthen the political power of the Islamic Republic of Iran by eliminating the opposition leaders. Even Amin, who did not want to be part of this terror plan, ultimately, because of his political convictions, decided to collaborate. There was not any specific order or obligation forcing them to assist in the plot.

Amin And Rhayel were even able to convince the accused, Atris. Atris became acquainted with Amin at the mosque, and he was Rhayel's co-worker at the Rosario restaurant. Atris frequently went to the Habibi restaurant, and it was there he made friends with the accused, Ataollah Ayad. But Atris and Ayad were not members of Hezbollah. Ayad had some experience at war, and he was the witness Adnan Ayad's nephew. Adnan was Darabi's brother-in-law and his business partner.

It is not clear why Atris and Ayad participated in the Mykonos terror attack, but their collaboration was also not based on a direct order or any kind of obligation.

Darabi talked Amin and Rhayel through the Mykonos attack plan as soon as they showed interest in it. Ayad also knew about the plan as early as July, 1992.

In a meeting at the Habibi restaurant where Amin, Rhayel, and the witness Jarade (who came to Berlin for the meeting from Phorzheim, a town in southwestern Germany, and the gateway to the Black Forest) were present, Ayad told them that the plan "would create a problem with the Kurds," a problem that could force him to return to Lebanon. So Jarade suggested that Ayad leave Berlin and stay in another city in Germany. Ayad opposed Jarade's suggestion, insisting that "this issue is a big one."

Ayad's anxiety was not rooted in his knowledge of the terror plan, it was because he was not ready to participate in the plot. Ayad was willing to help plan the terror attack, as long as he was not going to be a part of it. All Ayad knew was who was going to guard the restaurant's door, and who was going to drive the getaway car.

Late August, 1992, Amin, Atris, Rhayel, and Ayad were going to a party in Bad Homburg, organized in honor of the Moussa Sadre, the Shia's leader in Lebanon. Majdi Chahrour, one of Rhayel's and Atris's friends, accompanied them as well. Atris was driving the car, and he wanted to show off his driving abilities to the rest of the group. Atris had just been made aware of the plan to attack the Kurdish opposition leaders. He knew that, given expected levels of security, surprise would be necessary to successfully carry out the attack. Atris was ready and willing to participate in this evil plan.

At that time, it was decided that Amin would be armed with pistol and make sure the victims were dead, and Atris would drive the getaway car. Amin was probably uneasy about the role he was assigned to play. At that time, it was not yet clear what roles Ayad and Rhayel would play in the attack.

On August 25,1992, Darabi bought a mobile phone, for use as a second method of communication. He wanted to make sure he would be able to stay in touch with the rest of the team. He knew he would have to be responsible for the team, but in order to cover himself, he had decided to be out of town on the actual day that the murders took place.

The Terror Location

The location being considered for the terror attack, the Mykonos restaurant, was owned by Tabib Ghaffari.

Iranian opposition members were always organizing their meetings at that restaurant. If that was not immediately made clear to those planning the attack, at the very outset of their surveillance, it became clear, through information given to the regime's Intelligence agents, Ershad and Kamali, by one of their Kurdish informants.

The information became even more clear on September 1, 1992. During a meeting between opposition members, at the very same Mykonos restaurant, witnesses Dastmalchi, Jafari, Tabib Ghaffari, and other opposition members, talked about organizing a meeting with Dr. Sharafkandi. It was at that very meeting that Dehkordi announced that Dr. Sharafkandi would be coming to Berlin later in September.

The meeting finished with everyone in agreement that Dr. Sharafkandi would be responsible for taking the appropriate measures to ensure his own safety.

The Executive Hit Squad

The team, assigned by Fallahian, arrived in Berlin from Tehran around September 7, 1992. Abdolrahman Banihashemi was the leader of the team. He was also called Sharif, and the other team members knew him only by this name. Sharif was working for the Islamic Republic of Iran's Security Agency in Lebanon. He was the best man for the hit, because he knew Western Europe very well. He had previously led another successful hit, on the Iranian Pilot Talebi, in August, 1987, in Genova.

Another Iranian, named Mohammad, was also part of the hit team. Sharif, as the team leader, decided the details of the operation, and whether or not other measures would be necessary. He then connected with Darabi, in order to fulfill the task.

Darabi's role did not end with connecting with the hit team. He was also assigned tasks that needed to be performed by someone familiar with Berlin. Logistics, such as finding a safe house, guns, pictures of the victims, the getaway car, and assigning jobs to the team members, were all his responsibilities.

Banihashemi, leader of the hit squad, convicted in Mykonos Assassination

Assigning tasks and responsibilities to the team members had multiple purposes. In order to lead the operation in the best way possible, and guarantee its success, the local team had to support the hit team, both financially and logistically. In other words, the hit team should not have to expose themselves by staying at a hotel, connecting with the Iranian agencies, or finding guns for the operations. Moreover, the hit team had to leave the country where the crime took place, as soon as possible. The local support was also responsible for the tasks necessary after the operation. This is why the executive team and the local support are inseparable parts of an ensemble.

The success of the Mykonos operation depended on good coordination between these two teams. Therefore, Darabi had been involved in every little detail of this operation, from the beginning to the end.

When Sharif arrived, and took control of the team, he ended the involvement of Ayad and Atris. They were discharged from the operation because they were not members of Hezbollah. Darabi had to choose another one of his friends, Fazollah Haidar, resident of Osnabruck, to drive the getaway car, evacuating the hit men from the crime scene.

The rest of the details, such as what time the hit team would be arriving in Germany, were incumbent upon Sharif. According to the testimony of Klaus Grunewald, and the intel of the Federal Intelligence Service, even Mr. Mesbahi knew nothing about it.

About the Leader of the Hit Team, Mesbahi said, "When I was working for the Intelligence Ministry of Iran, I had heard things about Banihashemi. He is the leader of an operation team abroad. He had previously conducted the operation eliminating the Pilot Talebi, on August 18, 1987, in Genova."

Mesbahi explained how Banihashemi ran in to him, unexpectedly, in Tehran, and told him that the *"Kurdish issue"* was taken care of, under the secret name of "The Shia's loud outcry," and added that Fallahian had assigned him to the task. He also told Mesbahi that he had been the leader of the team, and had received an envelope. He did not mention anything about the content of the envelope, but for Mesbahi, it was clear that the envelope had contained the pictures of the victims. Banihashemi also told Mesbahi that he had been gifted a Mercedes 230 upon his return to Iran, as a token of appreciation for the success of his operation. Mesbahi witnessed, indeed, after this conversation with Banihashemi, that he left the premises driving such car. Mesbahi discovered later that Banihashemi had also become a share-holder in some fruitful financial operations. Mesbahi explained why Banihashemi would reveal such sensitive information to him; in that unexpected encounter, two other high-ranking members of the VAVAK were present.

The Court accepted the testimony of Mesbahi, because he gave the Court important and precise details about the way Banihashemi had escaped to Iran from Germany. Without any knowledge of Klaus Grunewald's testimony—that the hit squad left Berlin, after the operation and according to a very precise and prepared plan—Mesbahi told the Court that Banihashemi had escaped to Istanbul, encountering some issues in Turkey that made him very angry. He couldn't fly to Tehran directly from Istanbul, and had to drive to Ankara to catch a flight to Tehran. Mesbahi's testimony contained so many details that, without any doubt, they must have been described by Banihashemi himself.[34]

Amin's Move

Amin, who was living with his brother in Rhine, moved to Berlin shortly after his return from the Moussa Sadre's celebration, in early September, 1992. Berlin was where the local team, formed by Darabi, was awaiting the hit team. For reasons unknown, Amin traveled once again to Rhine, on September 10, 1992. Most likely, he wanted to see his wife, who was then expecting, one last time, before the operation in Berlin was to take place. Apparently, his return to Rhine had no impact on his decision to refuse to be more

---

34. Transcript of the Court, page 331

involved in the operation.

Preparation for the operation entered its final phase on September 11, 1992. Then, Amin was asked to return to Berlin. Rhayel called Amin to ask him to return to Berlin. Darabi also called him to emphasize the importance of his return. Darabi was respected by Amin, and he felt he owed Darabi, because of Darabi's kindness toward him. Therefore, Amin accepted his request, and came back to Berlin. Upon his arrival in Berlin, he resided at 64B Detmolderstraße, the safe house that Darabi had designated for the hit team. Sharif and Haidar were also staying there.

The Move to the Senftenberger Ring House

Darabi received the keys to the Senftenberger Ring House on September 12, 1992. This was the empty home of an Iranian student named Mohammad Eshtiaghi.[35] The house was located in Märkisches Viertel, in a 200-house neighbourhood. For this reason, it was very appropriate for the operation, without too much exposure.

Eshtiaghi was an Iranian student living in Germany, who had traveled back to Iran, for a short period of time, on August 28, 1992. Before leaving, he asked his friend, Bahram Berenjian, to look after his property, in his absence. Darabi knew Eshtiaghi, and taking advantage of his leaving, asked Berenjian for access to Eshtiaghi's empty house. Darabi then was able to relocate the team to Eshtiaghi's house and distance himself from what was to come.[36]

On September 13, 1992, Darabi held a meeting in his

---

35. Grünewald Memo, supra note 32, at 3; Indictment, supra note 34, at 27. That summer, Mohammad Eshtiaghi was traveling in Iran. He gave Brenjian a key to his house before he left. Id

36. Indictment, supra note 34, at 28; Mykonos Judgment, supra note 27, at 36

own house, at 64B Detmolderstrasseβe, with the Mykonos conspirators.[37] Banihashemi, Amin, Rhayel, Mohammad, and Haidar were present.

After the short meeting was over, Darabi assigned Rhayel to clean up the house and remove all evidence. Then he took the team to the new safe house, now established as the operational base, at 7 Senftenberger Ring in Berlin.

Darabi knew that after the terror attack, his house might be searched by the police. He planned to be in Köln or Hamburg on the actual terror day, giving him an alibi.

Rhayel cleaned the house thoroughly, but left a finger print of his left thumb on the inside of a glass closet-door; a very important piece of evidence, found by the police, after the attack.

Darabi then traveled, with his family, to Hamburg, on September 13, 1992. He checked into the Hotel Savoy, a little bit after midnight. Then, as planned, he was not in Berlin on September 17.

Buying the Getaway Car

On September 13, 1992, Ali Sabra, one of Darabi's closest friends, bought a car, from the witness, Oneri, at a second-hand car market. He paid DM3120.00 cash for a metallic blue BMW Series 7, registration number B-AR 5503. The money had been provided by Darabi, to procure transportation for the team.[38]

---

37. Anklageschrift, Der Generalbundesanwaltschaft Beim Bundesgerichtshof [Indictment, The Attorney General of the Federal Court] (May 17, 1993), at 27 [hereinafter Indictment]

38. Schluβbericht, Bundeskriminalamt [Final Report, Federal Criminal Police Office of Germany] (Aug. 22, 1993), at 5 and 16 [hereinafter Final Report]; Mykonos Judgment, supra note 27

Ali Sabra, showing a forged passport, presented himself as Mohammed Aslan, in order to purchase the car.
Rhayel and Haidar took possession of the car on September
16, 1992.

Choice of the Shooters

Banihashemi's plan was based on the presence of two
shooters; one with a machine gun, and the other armed with
a pistol. The shooter with the pistol had to make sure that
the victims were dead, that they could not be saved by any
possible intervention.

Initially, Amin was selected to be one of the shooters. When Sharif spoke with Amin about this, he was met
with refusal. Amin did not want the assignment, because of
his family situation, that he was going to be a father soon.
Sharif tried to make him change his mind, but Amin stood
his ground. Rhayel said he was being timorous. Amin did
not completely decline to participate, and agreed to watch
the door of the restaurant, during the operation. Rhayel was
then chosen to be the second shooter.

Passports for Escape After the Operation

The importance of Rhayel's role, making sure that the victims were dead, implied that his escape plan needed to be
thoroughly studied and prepared for. Therefore, Atris was
assigned the task of managing a passport for Rhayel. Atris
was fully aware of the plan for the attack, and, in his mind,
he had a clear picture of what was going to happen. He
knew that he was asked to prepare a passport for Rhayel,
because of the important role that Rhayel was going to play.
Atris knew that people were about to be killed. Whether he wanted these people to die or not is unclear, but he

agreed to participate and did what was expected of him. Atris promised he would take care of Rhayel's passport. He stole it from his own brother, Chauki Atris, who was living with him under the same roof. He therefore honoured his commitment.

The Arrival of the Representatives of the Democratic Party of Iranian Kurdistan to Berlin

On Sunday September 13, 1992, Nouri Dehkordi informed his wife, Shohreh Badiie, that their guests would arrive the next day.

Dehkordi and his wife had studied in Berlin, and then moved back home to Iran, after the Islamic Revolution of 1979. They had to escape from Iran in 1983, along with their daughter. They became political refugees in Germany. Dehkordi was a social worker in a refugee camp operated by the Red Cross. He was also very active politically, expressing his views openly on television, and protesting against the Iranian regime, specifically their policies regarding Kurds.

Dr. Sharafkandi had asked Dehkordi to participate in the Socialists World Congress, being held from September 15 to September 17, 1992.

Dehkordi was a trusted friend of Dr. Ghassemlou, although he himself was not even a Kurd, nor a member of the Kurdish Democratic party. But he was a supporter of their goals. He hoped for the opposition to unite against the regime, and force them to allow political diversity. This was exactly what Dr. Sharafkandi was looking for.

On September 14, 1992, in the evening, there was a gathering at Dehkordi's house. The witnesses Abdollah Ezatpour, one of the oldest members of the Democratic

Party of Iranian Kurdistan and the actual leader of the Party in Germany, Tabib Ghaffari, and Akbali, met at that event. Fatah Abdoli came over from Paris, and Homayoun Ardalan from Mainz. They discussed what was going to happen after the Socialists World Congress ended. This led to planning a meeting, between the representatives from the PDKI and members of other opposition groups, in Berlin. They planned to speak more about the political situation in Iran, and to decide on policies for the resistance against the regime in Tehran. On that evening, it was made clear that the meeting could not happen on September 18. The representatives of the Democratic Party of Iranian Kurdistan would be leaving Berlin for Paris on the morning of September 18, 1992.

The same night, Ezatpour, Abdoli, Ardalan, and Tabib Ghaffari, interrupted the gathering to go pick up Dr. Sharafkandi at the airport, at 9:30pm, and drove him to his hotel. Sharafkandi was flying in from Copenhagen. And Dehkordi had to attend to a television interview.

Invitation to the Meeting at the Mykonos Restaurant

The decision surrounding the location and time of the meeting between the representatives and the other opposition members was made on a Tuesday evening, September 15, 1992. Very late that night, at 1:00am, Dehkordi called Tabib Ghaffari, the owner of the Mykonos restaurant, and asked him to invite a list of 10 to 15 names to the restaurant for the meeting. Tabib Ghaffari did what Dehkordi asked, but he mistakenly invited people for Friday night, September 18, 1992 instead of Thursday, September 17, 1992.

Last Preparations for the Operation

Rhayel and Haidar, as assigned by Banihashemi, left the

house at 9:00am, on September 16, 1992, to pick up the guns. They returned a few hours later, with the guns in the trunk of the metallic blue BMW/B-AR5503. Banihashemi had ordered them to pick up the guns, wrapped in a paper box, and bring them to the house. The box contained a machine gun and an automatic pistol.

On the same day, the members of the team at 7 Senftenberger Ring were informed by a spy's phone call—the court never identified from who—that Dr. Sharafkandi would definitely be meeting at the Mykonos restaurant, with other opposition members, on September 17, 1992.

Under Banihashemi's leadership, Rhayel and Haidar were ordered to drive to the Mykonos restaurant, on September 16, 1992, at around 8:30pm, in order to familiarize themselves with the area around the restaurant. Sharif and Amin took the bus and the subway, exiting at Prager Platz, close to the Mykonos restaurant. At that location, a few moments later, Mohammad and an unidentified individual appeared, also in a Mercedes 190. The unidentified individual had had a role in the operation.[39]

The team left the area after having examined the situation and the paths that led to the location. They all returned to the safe house, on their own, where they spent the night of September 16, 1992.

Identifying the Victims

Regarding how terrorists identify their victims, we can refer to a report from the Iran group at the Bundesamt Für Verfassungsschutz (BfV), under the responsibility of Klaus Grunewald: "...necessary identifications in regard to the

39. Mykonos Judgment, supra note 27, at 41

personal details of the victim's life are made by the team, who usually travels for the preparation of the final phase of the hit on that person's life…"

The report that Grunewald presented to the Court, on April 22, 1993, stated that individuals from the Islamic Republic of Iran's Ministry of Intelligence had been in Berlin, and had identified the location of the terror attack.

Confirming this, Mesbahi learned, from some of his acquaintances, that Hadavi Moghadam and a cover company involved in this affair had done the primary identifications for this operation. Moghadam then activated his sources and released the information, and his suggestions, to Fallahian. Mesbahi later discovered, through talks he had had with these people in 1994, that two members of the research team had come to Berlin during the end of June and early July, 1992. According to Mesbahi, the research team's contact with the local people was made possible through a secret code.

The Secret Code: "The Outcry of the Shi'ite Religious Leader"

The Bundesamt Für Verfassungsschutz has mentioned this secret code as well in the report of the Iran's group. Mesbahi who was informed by Abdol-Rahman Banihashemi himself about this secret code told the court that this secret code meant "the leader of the Shia's will."

Mesbahi knew about the existence of secret codes given his own professional experience and said that secret codes were used to communicate until the final order for the terror is established.

Mesbahi testified in Court that in regards to the plan of terror of Hadi Khorsandi (1987-88), he heard the secret code from the deputy Minister of the IRI's Ministry of Intelligence, Reyshahri. It is worth mentioning that Mesbahi denounced this terror attack and prevented it from happening.

The logic behind Mesbahi's statement that the secret code is needed to conduct the operation until it is final, is understandable. Because as such, they can make sure that they have considered that any sudden changes in the situation can lead to the cancelation of the whole operation. According to Mesbahi, for any operation of this kind, a telephone line is established which disappears after the operations. Banisadr also confirmed this information in his testimony based on other sources.

The Operation

On the morning of September 17, Rhayel and Haidar went out to purchase a green and black Sportino sports bag, to be able to easily carry the weapons.[40]

Sharif went out shortly after Rhayel and Haidar had left the house. Rhayel and Haidar returned to the safe house at 4:00pm Sharif returned to the safe house at around 7:30pm and ordered everyone to pray. After the prayer, they waited for the phone call, that they were expecting to receive, from Mohammad. They had in their possession the pictures of the people they were supposed to assassinate.

The witness Böhm arrived at the restaurant at around 10:00pm He sat in the front room, facing the entrance. A young couple, not at all involved in the case, left the restaurant shortly after. Given that a young student, Ms. Voltschanskaya, was serving at the restaurant that night, Tabib Ghaffari, the owner of the restaurant, could sit and talk for a little while

---

40. Mykonos Judgment, supra note 27

140   with Dr. Sharafkandi and the other guests.

At 7 Senftenberger Ring, the phone rang at around
9:00pm That was the code between Banihashemi and Mohammad, who was keeping the restaurant under surveillance. It meant that the PDKI party had arrived and the
operation could begin.

Banihashemi started moving right away. He ordered
Rhayel and Haidar to go to the location, driving the BMW
to Prinzregentenstraße[41].

Banihashemi left the safe house with Amin, taking a
taxicab to Kurt-Schumacher-Platz. Then, they went into the
underground subway, left it by another exit, and went to the
taxi station close by, where they took another taxicab to another underground subway at Berliner Straße. Again, they
went into the subway station and walked out by another
exit. To make sure they were not followed, they walked to
the location of the restaurant from Geisbergstraße, although
it was still a long way from the Mykonos restaurant. They
met up with Mohammad near a public phone. Banihashemi
then separated from Mohammad and Amin, to check on the
other members of the team. Meanwhile, Amin and Mohamad kept walking around. When they reached Banihashemi, he was talking with the driver of a Black Mercedes
Benz 190. The driver, whose identity remains unknown,
drove off, after a short conversation with Banihashemi.[42]
Amin and Mohammad walked, at a discreet distance from
Sharif, toward the Prager Platz.

When they arrived at Prinzregentenstraße, where the
BMW was parked, Mohammad replaced Rhayel in the car,

41. Mykonos Judgment, supra note 27, at 48; Indictment, supra note 34, at 29

42. Indictment, supra note 34, at 19; Sachstandbericht, Bundeskriminalamt
[Summary of Facts, Federal Criminal Police Office of Germany] (Nov. 13,
1992), at 8 [hereinafter Summary of Facts]

and Banihashemi retrieved the sports bag, containing the intended murder weapons, from the trunk of the BMW. Rhayel and Banihashemi then armed themselves and started walking to the Mykonos restaurant, accompanied by Amin. A few seconds before arriving at the restaurant, Banihashemi told Rhayel and Amin that he had to go in first, Rhayel would follow, while Amin would stand at the door, preventing anyone from coming in.

Haidar and Mohammad waited in the getaway car at Prinzregentenstraße.[43]

Banihashemi and Rhayel entered the restaurant at around 10:50pm, and Amin closed the door behind them. They hid their guns so well that even the witness, Peter Böhm, did not see anything.

They continued their way toward the back of the restaurant where the party of nine were eating, and talking, and sensing none of the danger approaching. Banihashemi, who had pulled the collar of his turtleneck sweater up to just under his eyes, covering his face, started shooting the victims, shouting in Persian, "Son of whores!" He started shooting toward Dr. Sharafkandi, Dehkordi, Abdoli, and Ardalan. It was clear from where he directed his fire that Sharafkandi, Ardalan, and Abdoli, were the primary targets. In a few seconds, twenty-six bullets were shot, during two bursts of fire, from Banihashemi's Uzi. Tabib Ghaffari, the owner of the restaurant, sitting between Ardalan and Sharafkandi, got caught in the line of fire. He was shot through his right leg, and again through his kidney, but he survived the attack.[44]

Rhayel, who had followed Banihashemi into the room,

Darabi's Logistic Support

---

43. Indictment, supra note 34, at 29-30.

44. Mykonos Judgment, supra note 27, at 45-46; Indictment, supra note 34, at 31.

administered head shots to both Ardalan and Sharafkandi. He shot Ardalan once in the head, and Sharafkandi, twice in the head and once in the throat. Between the two assassins, they fired thirty shots in total.

Ardalan could have survived if Rhayel hadn't shot him in the back of his head. Banihashemi also shot Sharafkandi again, from less than five centimeters away, in the guts.

Sharafkandi was struck by twelve bullets in total, in his head, throat, guts, liver, and lungs. He was killed instantly.[45]

Ardalan was shot four times, in the chest, the abdomen, and the knee. Subsequently, the forensic examination revealed that he might have survived, if Rhayel had not shot him again, in the head and the neck.[46]

Abdoli was shot by four bullets from the Uzi. The one that hit him in the heart killed him instantly.

Dehkordi was hit by seven rounds from the Uzi. He was transferred to the Steglitz Clinic, where he died at 12:25am, due to hemorrhaging he underwent as a result of the bullets that hit him in the chest.[47]

The Getaway

After the operation, Banihashemi and Rhayel left the restaurant. Rhayel was still carrying the automatic pistol in his pocket, and Banihashemi carried the sports bag containing the Uzi machine gun. They joined Amin in front of the restaurant, and ran to the getaway car, parked at Prinzregentenstraße. Two other accomplices, Haidar and Mo-

45. Mykonos Judgment, supra note 27, at 46.

46. Professor Schneider, Direktor des Institut für Rechtsmedizin der Freien Universität Berlin [Director of the Institute of Forensic Medicine, Free University of Berlin], Mykonos Judgment, supra note 27, at 321-323.

47. Mykonos Judgment, supra note 27, at 46.

hammad, awaited them there.[48] Haidar was driving the car and, under stress, he almost hit a cyclist. In the car, Amin changed the coat and shirt he was wearing, and put them in a plastic bag so he could not be easily recognized.[49] Sharif ordered him to put the pistol, and Rhayel's knitted hat, in the sports bag as well.

Banihashemi and Rhayel exited the getaway car at the Bundesplatz U-bahn subway station.[50] Amin and Mohammad exited the car on Konstanzerstraße, at the corner of Hohenzollerndamm, and went in separate directions.[51]

They were supposed to meet again at the safe house. There is no information about what happened to Mohammad.

Amin didn't want to return to the safe house. While walking toward the underground subway at the Konstanzerstraße U-Bahn station, he dropped the plastic bag containing his clothes on the sidewalk. He continued on, toward Rathaus Neukölln (city hall in Berlin), to spend the night at his uncle's place, 160 Karl-Marx-Straße.[52] This was his official address. But when he arrived there, his uncle would not allow him to stay. He only allowed him to change his clothes, and leave. Therefore, Amin went to his friend Mohammad Abdollah's place, where he spent the night.

Haidar parked the car at 34 Cicerostraße, and left the Sportino sports bag, containing the murder weapons, hidden underneath a car that was parked in front of 33 Ciceros-

Darabi's Logistic Support

48. Final Report, supra note 37, at 7. See also Summary of Facts, supra note 42, at 9.

49. Mykonos Judgment, supra note 27, at 47.

50. Summary of Facts, supra note 42, at 9

51. Indictment, supra note 34, at 32

52. Mykonos Judgment, supra note 27, at 48

traße.[53] The Sportino sports bag, which contained the murder weapons used in Mykonos operation, was discovered on September 22, 1992, by the witness Wank, who was an employee of the Brolina car dealership.[54]

The weapons recovered in the sports bag were formally identified as a 9mm IMI machine gun manufactured by Israel Military Industries, model Uzi, and a 7.65mm Spanish Llama X-A Automatic pistol. There were also two silencers.[55] The German police traced the Llama automatic pistol, by its serial number, to a shipment purchased in 1972, by the Royal Army of Iran, from a Spanish provider.[56]

The two silencers could not be traced back to any official provider.

The forensic examination of the weapons revealed Abbas Rhayel's palm print on one of the pistol magazines, and traces of Nouri Dehkordi's blood on the pistol itself.[57]

The abandoned getaway car was towed to Schwartbachbrücke, by the police, just because it was illegally parked in front of the Brolina car dealership, and was blocking their door. Little did the police know, at that time, the connection this car had, to the murders at the Mykonos restaurant.

The car, towed to Schwartbachbrücke, was finally recognized as the Mykonos operation getaway car, following Amin's confession, on October 7 ,1992. The forensics then found, inside the getaway car, a spent 9mm Uzi cartridge, as well as a plastic bag with Amin's left index fingerprint on it.[58]

---

53. Indictment, supra note 34, at 32

54. Indictment, supra note 34, at 34; Mykonos Judgment, supra note 27, at 48

55. Indictment, supra note 34, at 34

56. Final Report, supra note 37, at 21

57. Indictment, supra note 34, at 34

58. Mykonos Judgment, supra note 27, at 48

Four suspects—Banihashemi, Mohammad, Haidar, and Sabra—escaped arrest. Banihashemi, the leader of the group of terrorists, escaped arrest, by boarding a flight to Turkey immediately after the assassination, and returned to Iran. Mohammad also left Germany, using his Iranian passport, and returned directly to Iran.[59] Haidar, the driver of the getaway car, returned to Osnabrück immediately after the assassinations. Then he escaped to Lebanon, from the Schönefeld Airport in Berlin, on September 25, 1992. Darabi was very anxious about Haidar. He called the witness, Feniche, to inquire about Haidar, and to ask whether or not he had already left Germany. Feniche reassured Darabi, in their last phone call, that Haidar had definitely left, with his family, to Lebanon. But when Haidar's wife connected, through a phone call, with the witness Maussa Hassen's wife, it was from a hotel in Tehran. Haidar has since been reported to be working for the Iranian Revolutionary Guards Corps.

The other suspected perpetrators were located, within a few weeks of the shootings, by German authorities, following the leads brought about by the German foreign intelligence service, the Bundesnachrichtendienst (BND).

Rhayel, the second shooter, spent the first few days hiding in Berlin.

Amin, who had guarded the restaurant's door during the assassination, left Berlin by train, on September 18, 1992. He went to Hannover, to a friend's house, and the next day he traveled to Rhine, to join his brother in the west of Germany.

Darabi, whose responsibility was to take care of the

Darabi's Logistic Support

---

59. Mykonos Judgment, supra note 27, at 48

members of the team of terrorists, came back to Berlin, from the witness Saghafi's place. He intended to meet with Haidar on September 18, 1992, to find out whether or not things had gone according to plan. Darabi tried to call ahead of his arrival, but as Haidar was not available, he went to see the witness, Feniche, their mutual friend who lived near Osnabrock, where Haidar had spent the night. Darabi left Feniche's place, early, on the morning of September 19. He arrived in Berlin at 8:00pm, on September 20. He talked on the phone with Haidar on September 23. No one knows the content of this phone call, but one day later, Haidar traveled to Rheine, where Rhayel had been heading as well. Whether the intended meeting between Darabi and Haidar happened or not is unclear, but Haidar went to Rheine to meet with Amin, on September 24, 1992. Haidar handed Amin DM2,000.00, on behalf of Darabi, and asked him to leave Germany as soon as possible. But Amin was not ready to leave.

As the anxiety surrounding the discovery of Rhayel's palm print on the pistol grew, Darabi suggested that Rhayel leave Germany, using the passport that Atris had prepared for him. Therefore, On September 24, 1992, Rhayel drove to Rhine, accompanied by Atris and the witness, Hussam Chahrour, and stayed there for a short period of time. At some point, Rhayel intended to depart for Lebanon from Amsterdam, so the three of them drove to Amsterdam together, to inquire about available flights. They wrote the information down on a business card and a piece of paper. Also, according to the witness Hussein Kanji, Rhayel inquired about the border between Germany and Holland, and if it could be crossed without being monitored by border control.

Rhayel finally met with Haidar, at Amin's brother's place in Rhine, on September 24. Haidar left Rhine after that meeting. Rhayel then begged Amin, multiple times, to leave Germany as soon as possible. Amin finally agreed, but he needed a passport with his picture, very quickly. Atris was able to help. On October 2, Atris left Berlin, accompanied by the witness, Chwaachou, to go to Rhine. Chwaachou's passport was supposed to be altered for Amin's escape. Rhayel's fake passport was ready for him on October 3, 1992, but Chwaachou's passport, with which Amin was supposed to escape, was not ready yet. Amin and Rhayel were arrested, ten minutes past midnight, on October 4, 1992, at Amin's brother's house, 17 Heriburgstraße, in Rhine.[60]

Darabi left Germany, flying from Hamburg, on September 27, to report to Tehran with the latest news. He also attended a wedding on October 1, 1992. Reassured, by events after the terror attack, that he could go back to Germany, Darabi bought a round-trip plane ticket to Hamburg, but left the return flight's date open. Having no knowledge of Amin's and Rhayel's arrests, Darabi flew back to Germany on October 4, 1992.

He found out about the arrests and decided to return to Iran, on October 8 or 9, 1992, but he was arrested at his house at 38 Wilhelstraße, in Berlin, on October 8, 1992.[61]

When Ali Sabra found out about the arrests of Amin and Rhayel, and saw their pictures in the newspaper, he was very anxious that he might be next, and decided to escape. He left Germany on October 20, 1992, without his family, from the Schönefeld Airport in Berlin. He returned to Lebanon where he is believed to be the guardian of the main residence of the Hezbollah spiritual leader,

---

60. Summary of Facts, supra note 42, at 17-18

61. Final Report, supra note 37, at 15 and 17

Sheilh Fazlollah.[62]

After hearing of the arrests, Ataollah Ayad found it more reasonable to leave Germany, but he needed money to buy a ticket, and a passport. So, he began calling friends for assistance.[63] First, he called the witness, Mehri, in Stuttgart, to inquire about a passport and money. Mehri refused to help him. Ayad then called the witness Mohammad Jaradeh, in Phorzheim, and told him he would visit him during the weekend, October 10 and 11, but he never arrived. Instead, Ayad called him again on October 25, explained his involvement in the Mykonos operation, and asked him for DM2000.00, to buy a plane ticket. In early November, 1992, in Heilbronn, a meeting took place between Ayad, Jaradeh, and the witness Chehade, who was the representative of Amal in Europe. Ayad explained, once more, the degree of his involvement in the Mykonos terror attack, and requested some money. He was again refused help, and was arrested on December 9, 1992, in a refugee camp, where he lived with his family.[64]

Atris was arrested on October 7, 1992.

62. Mykonos Judgment, supra note 27, at 51-52

63. Mykonos Judgment, supra note 27, at 104

64. Final Report, supra note 37, at 15

Chapter IV

Witness C:
Abolghasem (Farhad) Mesbahi

Witness C, subsequently identified as Abolghasem (Farhad) Mesbahi, was the key prosecution witness for the Mykonos trial.

Mesbahi was summoned by the Court, for the first time, on October 7, 1996. By the Court's decision, the session was not open to the public. Although the President of the Court reminded everyone that what was said in the Court that day would be strictly confidential, within a few days, the journalists knew everything about Witness C's testimony. Generally, while the Mykonos trial was in process, the totality of Berlin's Justice Palace was under strict security measures. The Attorney General of Germany, Mr. Kay Nehm,[65] personally ordered that Witness C be placed in witness protection, after his last testimony, on October 2, 1996.

---

65. Preceded by Alexander von Stahl

Mr. Nehm was concerned that Witness C might be "liquidated" by the Iranian regime.

Witness C, Abolghasem Mesbahi, was born in 1957, in Tehran. He graduated from high school in Tehran and signed up for the draft in 1977. He deserted a year later, around the beginning of the revolution, when Khomeini ordered that every serviceman abandon their posts. He was part of Ayatollah Khomeini's personal guard, in his motorcade, when he landed in Tehran, on February 1, 1979. From that day forward, he became the Chief of the Jamshidieh Garrison, Tehran's largest military base, by the order of Khomeini himself. Those days, a few of Iran's Royal Army's Generals, and other high-ranking officers, were kept prisoner in that garrison. Most of them were executed without trial.

Mesbahi left Iran, in the middle of 1981, to continue his education in France. He was then a member of The Ministry of Intelligence of the Islamic Republic of Iran, initially known as SAVAMA, when it took over the previous regime's intelligence apparatus. The ministry is one of the three "sovereign" ministerial bodies of Iran, due to the nature of its work at home and abroad.

Mesbahi's undercover name was Reza Omeidi, and his ID number was 1163. He travelled often, between Iran and France. In 1982, under the guise of a senior diplomatic attaché, he was in charge of the intelligence station at the Iranian Embassy in Paris. He settled his office on the third floor of the Embassy. His direct superior was a high-ranking intelligence agent, named Khosrow Tehrani. Mesbahi was also offered the title of Consul of Iran in France, which he refused, because he found himself *"too young,"* and not capable of assuming that rank. His activities were directed primarily against exiled opponents of the Iranian government.[66]

Mesbahi was declared *'persona non grata'* by the French authorities and expelled from France in early January, 1984, because his intelligence activities were discordant with his diplomatic status. He was deported after having been arrested on December 23, 1983, and detained, for ten days, by the French Police.

Nonetheless, one week after his expulsion from France, he returned to Europe through Hamburg, Germany. He was then transferred to the Iranian Embassy in Bonn, where he served as the intelligence coordinator for Western Europe, and continued to monitor the Iranian opposition.[67]

He was then constantly moving around, between Belgium, Luxembourg, Germany, and Switzerland. One of Mesbahi's responsibilities was to coordinate the different local units of the Union of Islamic Student Organizations and their activities in Europe. Since the Ministry of Intelligence of the Islamic Republic of Iran was founded, these Unions had become important bases for the Supreme Leader's network of intelligence activities abroad. During that time, Mesbahi was always in possession of 3 different passports, a diplomatic passport, a government passport, and a personal one, and he used them according to his needs.

In 1985, Mesbahi was summoned to return to Tehran, by Ayatollah Khomeini himself, to assist in assembling, along with a group of forty other individuals, the new Ministry of Intelligence.

At the time of its founding, the new Ministry of Intelligence used the Union of Islamic Students Organizations and mosques as important bases. In those days, two dif-

---

66. Mykonos Judgment, supra note 27, at 335

67. Mykonos Judgment, supra note 27, at 335

ferent factions formed. One faction believed that the MOI should only gather information to protect the country, but the other faction believed that the responsibility to eliminate enemies of the regime fell under their job description as well. Mesbahi believed in the first faction's ideas, that they could defeat the enemy with superior intelligence, but Khomeini and Fallahian found the idea of the second faction more appealing, and argued for bloodshed.

After having participated in the successful founding of the new MOI, Mesbahi officially worked for this ministry. In 1986, he served as the Deputy Head of the International and Political Office of Larijani (Foreign Ministry) for six months, and was then put in charge of the United Nations affairs desk. He was also Head of Strategic Studies of Europe and the United States within this Ministry. It was then that Rafsanjani—who was the head of Parliament at the time—became interested in Mesbahi, and sent him to Genova, Switzerland as a PhD candidate, where he acted as a back-channel for Rafsanjani's contacts with European governments.[68]

While in this position, he traveled to France, the United States, and Germany, and connected with French President François Mitterand, former U.S. President Ronald Reagan, the German Chancellor Helmut Kohl, and a former French Foreign Minister, Roland Dumas. All in an attempt to free 23 western hostages, taken by Hezbollah. He was successfully involved in freeing Rudolf Cordes, a West German hostage, working for Siemens AG, seized in Beirut by the Shi'ite group Holy Strugglers for Freedom. At this time, Mesbahi worked in close connection with Wolfgang Schäuble, then Chief of the Federal Chancellery; Erhard

---

68. Witness statement of Abolghasem Mesbahi (witness C) on Sep. 25, 1996

Eppler, a former Minister for Economic Cooperation; and Hans-Jochen Vogel, then Leader of the Social Democratic Party. They were members of a committee, created by the Chancellor's office, to conduct the hostage negotiations to free Cordes. Cordes was seized in January, 1987, and held until September, 1988. Mesbahi testified that the majority of these abductions had been ordered by religious authorities in Iran, and conducted by Hezbollah and Hamas operatives.

Mesbahi also acted as mediator between Ayatollah Khomeini and former U.S President Jimmy Carter, delivering Carter's letters to Khomeini.

Carter had advocated for the release of his long-time friend, Erwin David Rabhan, who had served as the pilot for Carter's first campaign for governor, in Georgia, in 1970. Rabhan is an American businessman from Savannah, Georgia. He was imprisoned in Iran for nearly eleven years, from September, 1979 until August 6, 1990. He was initially charged with breaking Iranian financial laws, and then later charged with spying, though he was never convicted. There is speculation that his arrest during Carter's presidency was connected to his association with the president, and was an attempt, by the Iranians, to punish Carter in a personal way.

Two of Carter's letters to the Ayatollah Khomeini were made public, by the Iranian authorities, on November 19, 1988. The pilot was released, and arrived in United States on September 14, 1990.

Mesbahi was arrested in November, 1988, upon his return to Iran, after having met with former U.S. President Jimmy Carter fourteen days prior, and delivering his third letter to Khomeini. Mesbahi was accused of being a double-agent, and thrown into solitary confinement, for 16 consecutive days, at Towhid prison. This prison is located in the basement of the Ministry of Foreign Affairs. He was released after three months, but remained under house arrest for another 18 months. Having been dismissed from the Ministry of Intelligence, he started a private business, to support himself.

Fallen from grace, it was his old friend, Saeed Emami, deputy to Minister Fallahian, who warned Mesbahi, on March 19, 1996, that the Special Affairs Committee had ordered his assassination.[69]

His last and only friend, Emami, told Mesbahi, "Do not go on vacation with your family. Leave the country! They want to "truckicide" you! Can't tell you how I know! That alone will kill you! Just go! Find a way to cross the border. Tell absolutely NO ONE you are leaving."[70] Banisadr told Mesbahi, later, when he was in Pakistan, about his own wife working for the secret services and spying on him.

Mesbahi left Iran for Pakistan, on April 18, 1996, with help from the chief of the largest tribe in the south. Mesbahi had once helped the chief get released, after being detained due to an unregistered gun. Stunned by Mesbahi's intervention on his behalf, the chief had vowed to return the favor if Mesbahi ever needed help. The chief accompanied Mesbahi personally, making sure he crossed the border safely into Pakistan.

In Pakistan, Mesbahi made asylum requests to several European countries, but they were all rejected. A record of deportation, from France in 1982, did not play in his favor. All the diplomats that he once knew now refused to help him.

---

69. Witness statement of Abolghasem Mesbahi (witness C) on Sep. 26, 1996

70. Book, Roya Hakakian's Assassins of the Turquoise Palace, at 237

Without anyone else to turn to, Mesbahi finally contacted the former Iranian President, Abolhassan Banisadr, every defector's last resort. Banisadr only agreed to help Mesbahi under two conditions; that Mesbahi tell all that he knew about the devil, Fallahian, and the Mykonos murders, and that he redeems himself, doing right by his own people.

After several inquisitions, former President Banisadr finally decided to help Mesbahi, who was then able to move to Germany, where he was granted political asylum.

Known to secret service officials, Mesbahi was the most senior operative to ever defect from Iran's Ministry of Intelligence. Given the tangible facts, and his measured and unsentimental authenticity when detailing characters and circumstances, one can have no doubt as to the important role Mesbahi must have had, within the Intelligence apparatus of the Islamic Republic.

The government of Iran claimed that Mesbahi had never had any connection to the Ministry of Intelligence. Their claim was merely an attempt to discredit Mesbahi, and his testimony about the Mykonos operation. Mesbahi's behavior during the depositions did not provide any reason to question the veracity of his statements. He made precise distinctions between what he knew from his own experiences, and what he had learned from conversations with other people, or from hearsay. In order to establish credibility for the information he received, he quoted the names of his sources, and their functions within the different state agencies.

Mesbahi said that, since the 1979 Revolution in Iran until then, 1996, in total, 95 opposition members had been murdered, in Western Europe, by the Iranian government. Every murder, without exception, had been ordered by the Supreme Leaders. The first victim of this terror was Shahriar Shafigh, a Royal Navy Captain, who was assassinated on December 7, 1979, in Paris. He was the son of Princess Ashraf Pahlavi, twin sister of the Shah of Iran, Mohammad Reza Pahlavi. The last victim, to that date, October, 1996, was Dr. Reza Mazlouman, Iran's former deputy minister of Education, who was assassinated in Paris, in May, 1996.

Mesbahi said that an attack on opposition members, either inside the country or abroad, is such a sensitive matter that it is never executed without a written and signed order. He testified in court that as long as Khomeini lived, every terrorist attack had been personally issued and signed by only him. Since Khomeini's death, any execution orders had been issued by his successor, the current Supreme leader, Seyed Ali Khamenei. According to Mesbahi, after Khomeini's death, sensitive matters of state, including, among others, suppression and physical elimination of political opposition to the Islamic Republic, is handled by a body named the "Special Affairs Committee" (komitey-é-omour-é-vijeh). Composed of eight permanent members, this committee is headed by the Supreme Leader, currently Ayatollah Seyed Ali Khamenei. The other members are the President of the Republic, the Foreign Minister, the Intelligence Minister, the Minister of the Interior, the IRGC's Commander-In-Chief, a member of the Guardian Council, and the head of the Islamic Republic of Iran's police. The Special Affairs Committee decides who has to die, so that the Islamic Republic can continue to live.

Once the Special Affairs Committee decided to liquidate a political opponent, operational responsibility for carrying out the Special Affairs Committee's instructions fell to the Special Operations Council, in the Ministry of Intelligence, at the Turquoise Palace. The Turquoise Palace Committee, headed by the IRGC's Commander-In-Chief, is responsible for the execution of the assassination order. The executive plan is then communicated, in two copies, to the Supreme leader and the President of the IRI. The executive plan, once reviewed by these two men, can receive the final approval.

Abolghasem Mesbahi testified that Abdol-Rahman Ghassemlou, leader of the Democratic Party of the Iranian Kurdistan, was assassinated in Vienna, in July, 1989, by the people who were sent to supposedly conduct talks and negotiations on behalf of the Islamic Republic of Iran. Given the fact that the PDKI was not dissembled by Ghassemlou's assassination, and that a new leader of the DPKI, Dr. Sadegh Sharafkandi, had replaced Ghassemlou for the party, the Special Affairs Committee made the decision, in 1991, to liquidate him as well. This time, Ali Fallahian, the Minister of Intelligence was chosen to oversee the operation. Ali Fallahian put his best operative, Abdol-Rahman Banihashemi to the task. Banihashemi's family had accompanied Khomeini in exile, in Najaf, Iraq. Abdol-Rahman had two other brothers. Abdol-Hamid Banihashemi was killed during the Iran-Iraq war, he was a member of the IRGC. Abdol-Madjid Banihashemi is a member of the IRGC and works in connection with Hezbollah. He lives in Lebanon.

Witness C testified about his sources: *"I have had five different sources, who are all high-ranking officials. One of them, Minister Fallahian's deputy, was directly involved in this terror operation, but he was not directly involved in the shootings. All these people are my close friends. My second source works in the Supreme National Security Council. The council operates according to Article 176 of the Con-*

158 *stitution.*[71] *My third source is a close relative of Ali Falla-*
hian, who had accompanied Asghar Arshad and Ali Kama-
li, traveling to Berlin on a mission to assess the feasibility
of undertaking assassinations in Germany. The fourth one
is a high-ranking member of the Ministry of Intelligence,
and the fifth one is a relative of Ayatollah Reyshahri."

Gajal Abdoli, Fatah Abdoli's spouse

---

71. The council was formed for the protection and support of national interests, Islamic revolution, territorial integrity and national sovereignty of the country. This institution was founded during the 1989 revision of the constitution.

Ceremony of installation of a memorial plaque for the victims of Berlin assassination in front of the Mykonos restaurant, Sara Dehkordi (Nouri Dehkordi's daughter), Hans - Joachim Erich, Fattah Abdoli's lawyer (with glasses, behind Sara Dehkordi)

The Memorial Plaque for the victims of Mykonos Assassination in Berlin

Witness C

Berlin court, April 10, 1997, the day of the verdict. In a 395-page
decision, the presiding Judge, Frithjof Kubsch, said: "Iran's political
leadership ordered the crime."

Berlin Court, Mykonos Trial verdict day, April 10, 1997
Germany's Concerns over Terrorist Acts

Interview With Parviz Dastmalchi

Avideh Motmaen-Far interviewed Parviz Dastmalchi in honour of the release of the English translation of his book, *Terror in the Name of God. The interview has been translated into English and is presented here.*

Question: The Islamic Republic has always claimed that the assassinations of opposition members, in Iran or abroad, are the work of rogue individuals. What is your take on that?

Parviz Dastmachi: This claim of the "arbitrariness" of assassinations started even before the rise of Islamic fundamentalists in Iran and is rooted in Shiite traditions in which lying is admitted in the form of *taqiyyah*.[1]

---

1. Taqiyyah, in Islam, is the practice of concealing one's belief and foregoing ordinary religious duties when under threat of death or injury. Derived from the Arabic word *waqa* ("to shield oneself"), *taqiyyah* defies easy translation. English renderings such as "precautionary dissimulation" or "prudent fear" partly convey the term's meaning of self-protection in the face of danger to oneself or, by extension and depending upon the circumstances, to one's fellow Muslims. Thus, *taqiyyah* may be used for either the protection of an individual or the protection of a community. Moreover, it is not used or even interpreted in the same way by every sect of Islam. *Taqiyyah* has been employed by the Shī'ites, the largest minority sect of Islam, because of their historical persecution and political defeats not only by non-Muslims but also at the hands of the majority Sunni sect. https://www.britannica.com/topic/taqiyyah

These fundamentalists have always had a monopoly on crime and incivility throughout Iranian history. Today, evidence shows that the perpetrators behind the 1978 burning of the Rex Cinema in Abadan, Iran—which killed more than four hundred innocent people—were the same "rogue" individuals who have since become high-ranking officials in the Islamic Republic, some even occupying seats in the Islamic Consultative Assembly. People such as Ayatollah Dori Najafabadi, former Minister of Intelligence and Security, who ordered serial assassinations of opponents inside the country; or Ali Fallahian, Minister of Information and Security, who ordered the Berlin assassination. They are members of the Assembly of Experts, the highest legal body designed by the Constitution of the Islamic Republic of Iran.[2] They are the people who appoint the "holy" leader of the system. People like Mostafa Pourmohammadi, Minister of Justice during the first term of the presidency of Hassan Rouhani, or Ayatollah Ibrahim Reisi, appointed Head of the Judiciary, controversial hardline clerics who are accused of gross human rights violations. These two clerics, at the head of "The Death Commission", have been directly involved in issuing the death sentences of about ten thousand political prisoners. These are things that happen when the system is a criminal system.

Question: What can you provide as evidence that proves the direct involvement of the Islamic Republic in the Mykonos assassination?

Parviz Dastmalchi: Abolghassem Mesbahi, the former Iranian intelligence officer who defected and escaped from the Iran during the Mykonos trial, testified as Witness C and told the court about

---

2. The Assembly of Experts—also translated as the Assembly of Experts of the Leadership or as the Council of Experts—is the deliberative body empowered to appoint and dismiss the Supreme Leader of Iran. https://en.wikipedia.org/wiki/Assembly_of_Experts

the assassination of dissidents inside and outside the country. He said that before the establishment of VAVAK in September-October 1985, there had been a series of assassins who carried out the direct orders of the Supreme Leader of the Revolution, Ayatollah Khomeini. The operations would not have taken place without Khomeini's approval. After the establishment of VAVAK, the assassinations were organized under the direction of the "Special Operations Committee" and supervised by the Minister of Information and Security. After Seyyed Ali Khamenei became the Supreme Leader in 1989, the "Special Affairs Council" was established, its authority higher than that of the government. This Council is tasked with decisions on all important matters, matters that are outside the authority and duties of a government due to judicial-religious aspects. Decision-making in this "Council" was not only related to the murder of dissidents, but also included, for example, closing the office of the Freedom Movement (Bazargan), which was delegated to the Ministry of Interior. The "Council" has both fixed and variable members. According to Mesbahi, when the issue of a murder is raised in the council, the decision must be approved by the Supreme Leader without exception, and no one is allowed to act without his order. Permanent members of the Special Affairs Council are the religious leader of the regime or his representative, Mr. Hejazi, and the President or his son. Usually, the Supreme Leader or the President do not attend ordinary council meetings in person. Other members are the Minister of Foreign Affairs, the Minister of Information and Security (VAVAK), the IRGC Commander-In-Chief, Commander-In-Chief of Law Enforcement, and a member of the Guardian Council who is also in charge of religious affairs of the council. Simply put, there has never been any "arbitrariness" at any time, but the decision to assassinate dissidents has always been and will always be made by the highest officials in the system, including the Supreme Leader himself.

Question: Well, doesn't this allow for the argument that some people may still have acted arbitrarily?

Parviz Dastmalchi: Let's suppose for a second that Mesbahi's statements are false and some people might have acted arbitrarily, for example, in the Berlin assassination. The Islamic Republic authorities first chose to ignore everything, and they then later confronted the undeniable documents regarding the interference of agents, diplomats, and representatives of the Islamic Republic of Iran. In the Berlin assassination, the IRI claimed that the perpetrators were rogue agents who had nothing to do with the official institutions of the Islamic Republic. Let's suppose this claim is true, and that Kazem Darabi and others acted arbitrarily, despite the fact that thirteen Iranian diplomats, including the ambassador, Seyed Hossein Mousavian, were expelled from Germany for good after the Berlin court ruled, and the German press reported extensively on the Iranian embassy's involvement in the European killings. So, why was Abdolrahman Bani Hashemi— the man who shot and killed four Iranian dissidents in the Mykonos restaurant—why was he not only not arrested upon his arrival in Iran, but also, according to credible court information, he was rewarded with a Mercedes-Benz 300 and a share in the profits of VAVAK cover companies? If Kazem Darabi, the organizer of the assassination in Berlin, acted "arbitrarily", then not only did he tarnish the reputation of the highest officials, including the Supreme Leader, but also irreparably damaged the country's interests. Why then, after his release from prison in Germany and his return to Iran, why is he not arrested and tried for complicity in the killing of four Iranian citizens, or for "arbitrariness" and playing with the regime's reputation? On the contrary, prominent State Department officials greeted him at the airport with a flower bouquet.

The same questions apply to Amin and Rahyel. Not only were

Hezbollah, but they were also welcomed into Iran as Darabi had been. Both later traveled to Iran, and nothing happened. The same is true of Ali Vakili Rad, one of the assassins of Shapur Bakhtiar and Soroush Katibeh. If he acted arbitrarily and discredited the regime, why, after his release from prison in France and his arrival in Iran at the airport, was he greeted with a bouquet of flowers by high-ranking officials of the Ministry of Foreign Affairs?

Most importantly: After it all—the court ruling, the conviction of the highest officials of the Islamic Republic of Iran, a 400-page sentencing document, a trial that lasted about four years and saw the testimony of more than eighty witnesses—members of the European Union, in solidarity with the court's decision, as well as with Germany, protested against the attacks perpetrated by the Islamic Republic and called back their ambassadors. European countries agreed to re-establish diplomatic relations only on the condition that Iranian officials pledge not to carry out any more assassinations on European soil. And the Islamic Republic agreed not to commit more murders on foreign soil. The Islamic Republic continued its assassinations until the condemnation in April 1997. The last ones were the murders of Dr. Sirus Elahi and Dr. Reza Mazlouman in Paris. The question is, if the assassinations were the work of "rogue" individuals, how can the government make a commitment not to conduct any assassinations and then be able to fulfill that commitment in this regard for more than twenty years? How is it that the "rogues" suddenly obey the will of the leader and the officials? In my opinion, what Abolghassem Mesbahi testified before the Berlin court is the truth: he said that the assassination of dissidents has always been carried out by order of the most senior officials, including the "holy" leaders of the regime, Khomeini and Khamenei, and without their agreement, no one dared to do such things.

Question: Is the role of the leaders of the Islamic Republic of Iran mentioned in the court ruling?

Parviz Dastmalchi: Yes, very accurately, the verdict states that "... the murder of Dr. Ghassemlou and two of his associates on July 13, 1989 in Vienna, as well as the murder that was examined in this court, are the results and consequences of the policies of the Islamic Republic of Iran. The connection between the Vienna and Berlin murders is very clear. The undeniable documents presented to this court, the type of decision-making of Iran's political leadership, as well as the structure and responsibilities of these decisions, which are aimed at destroying the regime's opponents abroad, are very clear. The decision to eliminate dissidents and opponents of the regime is in the hands of an institution called the "Special Affairs Council", which is an illegal body established by the order of the regime's religious leader. The members of this council are the President, the Minister of Information and Security, the Minister of Foreign Affairs, the heads of the military and law enforcement forces, as well as the religious leader of the system. The Berlin assassination was politically motivated and aimed at destroying the regime's opponents. The main goal of the Iranian regime is to eliminate active opponents of the regime abroad." Such a ruling is unprecedented in the history of Germany and perhaps in the world.

Question: Why do you think the regime kills its opponents?

Parviz Dastmalchi: In my opinion, the terrorism of the Islamic Republic of Iran has two main aspects, one is ideological and the other is aimed at maintaining power in order to gain status and wealth. The Islamic Republic of Iran is a fundamentalist Islamic order, like the Taliban in Afghanistan or ISIS, although of the Shiite type, because the Taliban and ISIS are Sunnis. From their point of view, non-Muslims can be killed, because that is the command of God. The fundamentalists consider "Jihad" for Islam and God as a duty, they think that Jihad has a reward and they will go to heaven.

Islamic terrorism has a long history in Iran. For example, about a hundred years ago, they assassinated the great Iranian thinker Ahmad Kasravi for criticizing Islamic superstitions. When the Islamic Republic took office, a memorial stamp was issued with the image of Nawab Safavid, the leader of the Fadaiyan-e-Islam, Kasravi's assassin. Look at the commemorative stamps for Captain Islamboli, the killer of Anwar Sadat, or the stamps commemorating the occupation of the US embassy in Tehran, which was against international law.

The second aspect of the Islamic Republic's assassinations of the opposition is a desire to maintain power. The regime, which is under intense pressure from both inside and outside, has intensified its policy of terror and repression. In order to survive, the regime has to intimidate people. Inside, union activists, union leaders, and lawyers are arrested and imprisoned, brutally murdered, or burned to death. For about two years now, activists have been reporting that the intelligence services had repeatedly summoned and intimidated them. Abroad, also, they have re-launched their assassination machine, starting about three years ago. Fortunately, due to US and Israeli pressure on Europe, their plans have failed. Plus, Europeans themselves are sensitive to terrorist activities. Of course, in Iraqi Kurdistan, the opposition is attacked with long-range missiles, and the Islamic Republic has no problem admitting, "Yes, we did it and we will do it again." But in Europe, the stakes are much higher if they get caught. So, when they are caught there, they deny everything and play the game that some "rogues" were involved.

Question: Does the Islamic Republic get help from non-Iranians for assassinations?

Parviz Dastmalchi: Yes, it depends on their capabilities and on how plausibly Iran can deny involvement. For example, in January 1980, a Lebanese terrorist named Anis Naghash was sent on a mission by the Islamic Republic of Iran. He tried to assassinate Shapour Bakhtiar. Bakhtiar survived, but a woman living next door to Dr. Bakhtiar's apartment was injured, a police officer was killed, and another police officer was paralyzed and died in 2008. The Lebanese-born Anis Naghash is a Sunni architect who later converted to Shiism. Following this unsuccessful assassination, Anis Naghash was arrested, tried and sentenced to prison. Following the efforts of the Islamic Republic of Iran, Naghash was released from prison after 10 years and moved to Iran, where he lives now. He has officially confessed to the failed assassination in some interviews in Iran. The question is, if IRI had no role in this assassination attempt, why do not they take any legal action against a person who officially confesses to the attempted assassination of another Iranian citizen?

Or looking at another example, the assassination of Ali Akbar Tabatabai in Washington, DC. Daoud Salahuddin, also known as Hassan Abdul Rahman or Hassan Tantai, is an African-American Muslim citizen who shot Ali Akbar Tabatabai, a former Iranian press attaché in Washington D.C., in front of his home in July 1980. Daoud Salahuddin was disguised as a postman. With three bullets, he killed Tabatabai, and then he fled to Iran. His real name is David Theodor Belfield, he was born and raised in New York and arrived in Iran after the July 1980 assassination. He married an Iranian woman and now speaks Persian. Remaining in Iran for more than thirty years, he became an English teacher and the head of the editorial board of Online Press TV (English-language news television of the Islamic Republic of Iran, based in Tehran). He also joined the "reformist faction". He says that he has never received any money from the Iranian authorities, other than the five thousand dollars he received for Tabatabai's assassination. "I arrived at Tehran's Mehrabad airport a week after Tabatabai's assassination," he said. He had been promised that if he had to flee, he would be sent to China for ten years to study traditional Chinese medicine at the expense of the Iranian government. They did not keep their promise. Salahuddin reported to the embassy of the Islamic Republic in Geneva just 48 hours after the assassination of Tabatabai. Ordered by Seyyed Ahmad Khomeini, the leader's son, Salahuddin obtained a visa and arrived at Tehran's Mehrabad airport nine days after Tabatabai's assassination. From there, he was taken straight to see the then Minister of Foreign Affairs, Sadegh Qutbzadeh. He visited Ayatollah Khomeini at his home in Qom in the late 1980s, and Khomeini told him personally: "The subject of that man in Bethesda (Tabatabai's residence) was in the way of Islam." All this was revealed by David Belfield himself in an interview with the Washington Post.

And of course, in the Berlin assassination they used Lebanese nationals as well. The two Lebanese shooters were members of Hezbollah and were trained in Iran, as was the guard at the restaurant's entrance. Several other non-Iranians, Arabs and Turks who were also involved in the Mykonos assassination, fled first to Lebanon and from there to Iran.

Question: The regime has not carried out any assassinations on EU soil for some time, why do you think they have started again?

Parviz Dastmalchi: The reason why they did not carry out any assassinations in the territory of the European Union from 1997 onwards, until three years ago, was that after the verdict of the Mykonos trial on April 10, 1997 and the conviction of the officials of the IRI as the masterminds of the assassination, many EU countries recalled their ambassadors from Tehran, severing diplomatic relations with Tehran. Germany could not allow another country to violate its sovereignty and carry out assassinations on its soil. Feeling this pressure, the IRI vowed to no longer carry out assassinations on EU soil, but then resumed three years ago, this time using mafia and criminal groups as henchmen. In Turkey, for years, they have used criminals, drug mafia and smugglers to either assassinate Iranian dissidents or kidnap and transfer them to Iran. A few months ago, a group of 13 Turkish criminals and traffickers was arrested and charged with kidnapping and murder committed in the name of the Islamic Republic of Iran. In the Netherlands two years ago, criminal gangs commissioned by the Islamic Republic assassinated Ali Motamed. It is said that the IRI paid 130,000 Euros for this assassination. But since the EU countries are now struggling with the problem of Islamic fundamentalist terrorism on their soil, they are no longer willing to ignore such assassinations, and they severely punish the perpetrators.

Question: Is the use of criminal gangs a new way of assassinating opponents?

Parviz Dastmalchi: You see, since the inception of the Islamic Republic in Iran, the Islamic fundamentalists have not respected domestic or international laws and obligations. The Iranian regime is a rebellious and criminal enterprise that has turned the structure of a government into a tool of internal and external terrorism. Contrary to all international laws and commitments, they occupied the US embassy in Tehran, held American citizens hostage for 444 days, and this was supported by the Supreme Leader. At the very beginning of their rise to power in Iran, they executed hundreds of people without trial. Political prisoners have since been massacred in numbers estimated between 5,000 and 10,000. They kidnapped writers and intellectuals, killed them and dumped their bodies somewhere. That was the case in the murder of the two Iranian writers, Mohammad Mokhtari and Mohammad Jafar Pooyandeh. Their assassin, Mehrdad Alikhani, confessed that the then Minister of Intelligence and Security, Ayatollah Ghorban Ali Dori Najafabadi, had ordered the assassination. He said that Mokhtari was kidnapped in the street, forcibly put into a car, and taken to the cemetery Behesht Zahra. In a pre-designated room, he was laid on the floor, handcuffed, blindfolded, and suffocated with a piece of rope taken from a cabinet inside the room. Alikhani confessed that he had to tighten the rope around Mokhtari's neck for about four or five minutes in order to suffocate him. Mokhtari's body was placed in the trunk of a car which was later abandoned on a side street. They did the same thing with Mohammad Jafar Pooyandeh. They kidnapped him, took him to Behesht Zahra, strangled him with a rope, and threw his body in a quiet street. This regime is criminal and whenever it could not formally commit a crime, it committed such crimes informally.

Question: It seems that in recent years, the Islamic Republic has changed its policies. It kidnaps dissidents abroad, transfers them to Iran, and sometimes executes them. What are your thoughts on this?

Parviz Dastmalchi: These acts are all signs of an arbitrary and lawless regime. Their new method of eliminating the opposition is to kidnap someone outside and then take them to Iran. They officially declare that they do this in order to both intimidate the opposition and show their power. Also, it is less costly to their reputation in the international arena. Whenever it better suits the IRI's propaganda, the abductees are also tortured into making false confessions. They are shown on television confessing to spying for foreign countries, given a sham trial, and then executed. The regime's officials confess to kidnappings and violations of civil rights and human rights, as well as violations of international law and the sovereignty of other countries. The Islamic Republic is a rebellious regime that constantly violates its international obligations and lies to everyone. This regime is full of hypocrisy.

Look at the current head of the judiciary, Ebrahim Reisi, who is one of the four accused in the 1988 political prison massacre.

Look at Hojjatoleslam Ali Fallahian, Minister of Intelligence and Security, as well as a member of the Assembly of Experts (who appoints the Supreme Leader), who has two international arrest warrants against him, one from the German prosecutor in connection with the Berlin assassination and the other from the Argentine prosecutor in connection with the explosion of the Jewish Cultural Center in Buenos Aires.

The assassins of Abdul Rahman Ghassemlou, the leader of the Kurdistan Democratic Party of Iran, who was assassinated in Vienna in July 1989 while negotiating with representatives of the Islamic Republic, were Haj Ghafoor Darjezi and Mohammad Jafari Sahraroudi. One of them later became one of the heads of state radio and television in Iran and the other became the chairman of the Islamic Consultative Assembly.

Question: Are the diplomatic missions of the Islamic Republic of Iran involved in such terrorist acts abroad?

Parviz Dastmalchi: Yes, a lot. Such assassinations or kidnappings require large-scale preparations—money to find weapons and safe houses, plans for the perpetrators and assailants to flee—and this issue was raised in both the trial for the attempted assassination of Shapur Bakhtiar and in the Mykonos trials. In a Berlin court, Mr. Abolghassem Mesbahi, known as Witness C, stated under oath that the Ambassador of the Islamic Republic of Iran, Mr. Hossein Mousavian, was involved in most of the assassinations in Western Europe and Germany. Newspapers also wrote about this. Mesbahi has been at the head of the regime's terrorist organization in Western Europe, and he knows what he is talking about.

Also By Mehri Publication